Sermons of John Slater

Sermons of
John Slater

Selected and edited by
Andrew Walker

with an introduction by
Mark Oakley

Covenanters

Published by
Covenanters Press
an imprint of
Zeticula
57 St Vincent Crescent
Glasgow
G3 8NQ
Scotland.

http://www.covenanters.co.uk
admin@covenanters.co.uk

ISBN-13 978-1-905022-29-8 Paperback
ISBN-10   1 905022 29 8 Paperback

Contents

Foreword

This selection of sermons by John Slater is offered in part as a tribute to him and to his ministry in London over many years but also in part because he was a fine preacher and many of his friends and former parishioners felt a collection of his thoughts and words would be a useful resource. Perhaps for the preacher looking for occasional inspiration or a different way of looking at or understanding some seasonal feast; perhaps for the layperson wanting some inspiration or fresh approach to faith in private reading; perhaps for a confirmation candidate or parish group who might want material for discussion.

While John tended to type and preserve his sermons they are rarely dated but the churches and institutions for which they were written are more frequently named. These range from the London parishes in which he served – All Saints' Margaret St, St Saviour's Warwick Avenue, St John's Wood and St George's Hanover Square – to include as well King's College in London, Christ's Hospital in Sussex, Union Theological Seminary and St Thomas' Fifth Avenue, both in New York. He always headed his sermons – both with a title which I have included here and with a Latin dedication which I have not, usually either *Ad Maiorem Dei Gloriam* or *Laudabo Nomen Domini* but very occasionally *Domine Exaudi* or *Deus in Adjutorium*.

As John himself commented every preacher has their dominant themes. His might perhaps best be summed up in some words from an early sermon:

If any word can be said to sum up the teaching of Jesus in the Gospels it is surely the word *metanoia*, which means a complete turn around in our view of the world and our way of living. We tend to translate it by 'repentance' or even sometimes 'being born again' but both are lame because they use an exclusively religious term of reference. We shall not convert others by theology; we shall not transform the world unless theological truth is enfleshed in a completely new way, both in the language and concepts we use and in the way we try to live our lives. It is we ourselves who must be the mirror in which others can see the image of God; and by seeing the world in a new way be themselves changed to reflect the glory of God.

To that task of enfleshing theological truth freshly John committed himself,pressing into service novels, films, contemporary writers and historical figures, scientific insights and philosophical developments. Even during his last years of illness he maintained his commitment to the task of preaching and to the adventure of fresh theological exploring and explaining. Would that we might all do the same! Finally I should say I am enormously grateful to Mark Oakley, a former curate of John's and now Archdeacon of Germany and Northern Europe, for his Introduction to this collection and to Anders Bergquist, John's successor as Vicar of St John's Wood, for supplying the biographical note that comprises the postscript.

Andrew Walker
Director of the London Centre for Spirituality,
and rector of St Mary Woolnoth in the City of London

Introduction to John Slater's sermons

For John Slater a sermon was not a script but an event and, consequently, I have very strong memories of John's preaching. To read this collection brought many of those memories back to me along with, I am not ashamed to say, some tears as well. Reading these sermons made me realise again how much I miss him and how much I owe him. It also brought home to me how, in those final days of his life, I tried to tell him just how important he was to me and to many of his friends, and how that mixture of modesty and self-doubt of his made it so difficult for him to hear.

John was never at his best trying to hear good things about himself. He was much happier behind a lectern or in a pulpit and ensuring that his priesthood was pointing at God and not him. He preached with passion, as if each sermon might be his last, with that intriguing voice that had captured something of his time in New York. He strained and pushed his voice to emphasise and educate, forging his way through historical insights and philosophical questions, Jungian interpretations and artistic expressions, to share his discovery that the Gospel of Jesus Christ is the way to enlarge our humanity and restore it back to a life worthy of the name. John's sermons reflected something deep within him – his desire to think critically and live faithfully.

He always said that the Sunday liturgy was the highlight of his week. This was translated into the way he presided at the eucharist and it was always visible when he came to deliver his sermons. He had the necessary joy of a preacher. His words, always carefully chosen so as not to resort to cliche or stale abstraction, lived, danced and hummed with resonance. A good preacher will always intrigue his or her hearers enough to step up on the diving board in an invitation to plunge deeper into the mystery and currents of God. John rarely failed to do this. As we listened we were aware of how much we didn't know or had never explored. We were brought face to face with things that amused and/or frightened. We were also aware that these words were authentic, acquainted with experience and hurt as well as with learning, and that they would never rest content with easy certainies or the seduction of quick clarity. They were words trying to pave a way towards the Kingdom of God. They were not from that other realm known well to some orators – what the Australian poet Les Murray calls "the Kingdom of Flaunt".

John was always sensitive to those to whom he was preaching, not least their personal wounds. I remember him warning me once about a sermon I had preached that spoke of a particular pain I had never gone through but which some in the congregation had. He was worried that preachers at such times simply add insight to injury, bearing down rather than alongside. I have remembered this ever since.

I often thought that John's sermons were capable of turning our theological and psychological full stops into commas. He had a high doctrine of the church and the necessary high doctrine of the Holy Spirit to go with it. He was not comfortable with change but neither was he afraid of it. Indeed, he often quoted Newman: "To live is to change and to be perfect is to have changed often". I know how many parishioners felt that they were on a journey with John through his preaching amongst them. They recognised their own longing for God within John but they also knew that he was leading them like the captain of a ship who can smell the land ahead before it is visible. Even the questions he raised without any closure were part of this priestly compass. He taught the truth suggestively not dogmatically. He went gold digging in the scriptures but read them as one might read a letter from a friend, reading the love between the lines and not in a literal dissecting of each word or phrase.

A friend of mine recently found herself talking to an Oxfordshire farmer and shepherd. She was intrigued as to how he actually used his shepherd's crook. Did he use it to hook a sheep's neck or to prod the lazy one? No, he said, he rarely did that. He found that he used the crook most of all by digging it firmly in the ground in front of him and using it to keep himself very still. This way the sheep learnt to trust him and were more inclined to be guided and led to where they were bound. This was John's style of shepherding. He was not particularly good at striding out front and expecting people to follow and decisions could be a long time in the making. His crook, however, was firmly rooted and those of us who had the joy of grazing nearby knew that his reliability and thoughtfulness would never let us down or desert us.

The Anglican divine Lancelot Andrewes once said in one of his Ash Wednesday sermons that "our charge is to preach to men *non quae audire, sed volunt audisse*", not what for the present they would hear but what in another day they would wish they had heard. John approved of this.

John was unapologetically a Catholic Christian, shaped at a time when Rome and Canterbury flirted with hope rather than just politeness. He was Catholic in that he believed the Church of England he served was a part of God's church and by him having a relentless capacity for friendships, believing Christian identity is intrinsically relational. Miroslav Volf once defined a catholic personality as one "enriched by otherness, a personality which is what it is only because multiple others have been reflected in it in a particular way". I was awakened again in reading these sermons to see how John infused the wisdom of mentors to make something very much his own. What he made, though, he offered for the good of the Church. It never became the basis of a personality cult.

One of John's favourite hymns, in fact probably his favourite of all, was Edmund Morgan's "You, living Christ, our eyes behold". The second verse reads:

Your glorious feet have sought and found
Your sons of every nation;
With everlasting voice you sound
The call of our salvation;
Your eyes of flame still search and scan

The whole outspreading realm of man:
Lord Christ, we see your glory."

John preached and lived seeking and blessing the glory of his God. He was a humane, cultured, fun, faithful priest and friend. He was sensitive, sometimes tentative and cautious in intimacy. He was social and party-going as much as he was protective and solitary. He was inspirited by that "whole outspreading realm of man" in which God's glory lay both hidden and unveiled. Most of all, perhaps, he wanted to teach, provoke, explore and journey with his friends and colleagues through that Christian conversation he initiated in his preaching and ministry. He fed, and was fed, by this calling he responded to with all the innocence and fire of a first love.

I want to thank Andrew Walker for assembling such good examples of John's sermons. Like me, Andrew heard them week in and week out as John's curate in St John's Wood Church. He was the right person to put this collection together and I know how grateful John's friends will be for his work and discernment.

As I watched John near the end of his life, living with so much discomfort, I was humbled but not surprised by the fact that the last thing he would give up was his preaching. With hardly any breath he drew on what little he had left to deliver sermons grounded in that pilgrim faith and resilience that had inspired so many and which had gained him so much love and gratitude. I had the privilege of anointing him near his death, anointing the priest who had taught me as a curate how to anoint the dying, and with no words left he simply made the sign of the cross. It was a beautiful, poignant, painful moment. And I have no doubt that a little later he began to sing again, with full breath, to the Living Christ whose glory he beheld at last.

Mark Oakley
Archdeacon of Germany and Northern Europe
and chaplain to St Alban's Copenhagen

1. Catechesis: Church and Sacraments

On the Church

The Church necessarily has both an outward and an inward aspect. Sometimes its exterior is frankly unattractive and so very unlike its Lord: proud where he was humble, triumphalist where he was crucified, compromised by establishment where he was fearless in his critique of both religious and political leaders. But the Church is more than its exterior face; it is the fellowship of all, past and present, who consciously or unconsciously unite themselves to Jesus Christ as the one in whom the meaning of our existence is to be found.

Part of the problem is the co-existence of the community of sinners with the communion of saints. It is not always easy to reconcile the great claims made for the Church theologically as 'the body of Christ' with the reality of what we encounter in its local manifestation in space and time. Even here though we need to avoid the temptation to the dualism that says spiritual things are good and material things are bad. Both aspects of the Church are true and provide both the vision and the location of what Dietrich Bonhoeffer so marvellously called 'costly discipleship.'

The Church is the fellowship of those who know Jesus Christ and it is within that fellowship that Christ is made known and his presence celebrated in word and sacrament. Bonhoeffer entitled one of his books 'Life Together' and that, I think, is what I want to say about the Church; it is life together – together with Jesus Christ our Risen Lord, together with all men and women who seek to follow his way, united to him morally, sacramentally, mystically.

On Baptism

Ritual washing is common in Old Testament law and there the emphasis is upon ritual cleanliness. Certain actions make a man or women impure and before they can resume their place in the community they must wash in a ritual way. By the time of Jesus baptism had become the ritual through which a gentile might become a member of the Jewish people; and there were a number of Jewish communities which practised daily ritual washings as a sign of their preparedness for the coming of the Messiah.

Then, of course, there is the baptism of John. He is linked to those eschatological communities which awaited the coming of the Messiah. But instead of daily washing he preached a once and for all baptism as the outward sign of a deep inner conversion to the ways of God. His baptism recalled the Exodus itself when the people first left behind the slavery of Egypt and crossed the Jordan to enter the Promised Land. John had candidates for baptism come to him from the eastward bank of the river, the land that was not the Land of Promise; confessing their sins they were submerged in the waters of the Jordan and they came out on the opposite bank of the river, so entering the Promised Land and a new relationship with God.

It is likely that after the resurrection the disciples of Jesus continued to baptise in the manner of John – proclaiming the possibility of a new relationship with God for those who repented of their sins and who confessed Jesus as Messiah and Lord. But Paul was to give baptism a new meaning. His own experience of conversion and faith, of Jesus and the Holy Spirit, led him to speak of living in Christ. So Christian baptism became the sign of entering a new relationship with Jesus, of becoming identified with him in his death and in his resurrection, and of being filled with the same Holy Spirit which descended upon Jesus in the form of a dove when he was baptised.

It is interesting that at first post-baptismal sin was thought to be unforgiveable – the sin against the Holy Spirit. Therefore baptism, as in the case of the Emperor Constantine, was often postponed until just before death. But the Church learnt from experience and a system of penance was developed for sinners to be restored to Christian fellowship. And here is one of the essential elements of our Tradition – it develops with the changing conditions in which the Gospel is proclaimed and the Christian faith is celebrated.

On Confession

Christians must sharply distinguish between guilt and penitence. Guilt is the result of a failure to live up to the standards set by ourselves or others. Unaddressed, it can lie at the heart of emotional breakdown and personal disintegration. Penitence is totally different and, in a creative response to vision and insight, leads always to liberation. These two possible responses to human limitation and failure are well exemplified in the respective reactions of Judas and Peter. Both 'went out' from the presence of Jesus. Peter went out and wept and came back again; Judas went out and destroyed himself. Penitence is at the heart of Christian maturity for it allows us to grow through our experience of failure, sorrow and tragedy.

The actual rite of confession is essentially part of the everyday domestic life of the Church. It is especially important at critical times – confirmation, sickness, serious sin, death – but it shouldn't be seen as something exceptional. For ultimately it is a way of confessing Christ, of personal surrender to him, of entering into an ever more intimate relationship with him. For Isaiah penitence is the result of vision and leads directly to restoration and then call. So the context of confession is twofold. On the one hand there is the community - for no one is an island and our sins as well as our virtues affect all other members of the body, be it the Church or our society. On the other hand we have the living out of our baptism in the pattern of encountering the continuing vision of Christ and the Gospel, the resulting need to offer penitence, the experience of ongoing forgiveness, and thus to renewed vocation.

Confession means to regard Jesus rather than myself, and then to see myself beside him, in the light of his love. This then is to have to acknowledge myself as unworthy, as falling short, but at the same time to experience myself as accepted and redeemed, as his love is slowly perfected in us.

On Marriage

All sacraments are signs of course. And as well as the giving and receiving of a ring in marriage being the sign of the inward grace of the union of man and woman in one flesh, so marriage is also a sign of the interpenetration of our mundane world by the Kingdom of God   For the Kingdom of God is not some future land we cannot yet see, but rather the human life we already know, lived in obedience to God's will. When a man and a woman live faithfully and lovingly together in accordance with God's will there is his Kingdom. And where marriage vows are broken we turn away from God's Kingdom. Though none of us can cast the first stone in those situations – which of us has not failed in respect of the fundamental vows of baptism – to turn to Christ, to repent of our sins, to renounce evil?

Baptism sets our feet upon the journey to God's Kingdom. On the journey we need nourishment and we are fed in the eucharist. We need confirmation that we are on the right path. We need teachers to direct us and pastors to draw us back when we have wandered from the way and healers to dress our wounds. Marriage in all this is the sacramental sign that we do not travel this way alone but in companionship, a companion being one with whom we share bread on the journey. So marriage can speak to us all, not only to those who are married.

The goal of the journey is not a land but a relationship – union with God in love. Experience teaches us that we cannot fully enjoy life until we truly love. If marriage is the model of ultimate human love, the forum for sacrifice and fulfilment and so partaking something of the nature of divine love, it nevertheless must point beyond itself to the broader love of others and the deepest love for God alone. In the Greek Orthodox marriage ceremony crowns are held over the heads of the bride and groom because they fulfil the divine purpose of creation which is self-giving love – united both to each other and to the Lord of all. In the ecstasy and joy of a wedding day we are all touched by that vision of dual union.

On Priesthood

By our baptism we are made members of the Body of Christ, sharing his priestly character and work. But that priestly character and work gain sacramental embodiment and expression in those who are set apart by ordination. The ordained priest is not there to monopolise priesthood in the Church, but to be a symbol of it, reminding all the members of the community that they share the priesthood of Jesus Christ and have a priestly task to perform in the world. The ordained person is a priest within the Church and with a mission to the Church; the Church is a priestly community within the world and with a mission to the world.

Behind the idea of priesthood is always the notion of representation, of doing something on behalf of others. Jesus dies on our behalf, performing a sacrifice for us, as our representative. In our turn, we represent the world in a response of thanksgiving to God for his redeeming work in Jesus Christ – so we are, by definition, a eucharistic community. Every eucharist we offer is not only on our behalf but on behalf of the whole Church and of the whole creation.

In the past, perhaps, the place of the ordained priest was emphasised at the expense of any sense of the priestly nature of the People of God as a whole, the priest being *alter Christus*. Today, perhaps, we tend to the other extreme and are in danger of losing the essential symbol and focus which the ordained person provides by giving sacramental expression to the priestly nature of the whole Christian community. In chapter twelve of his first Letter to the Corinthians St Paul writes eloquently about the diversity of gifts which the Holy Spirit pours out upon the Church. We each have different gifts and so also different ministries within the body – but none are sufficient unto themselves, all are interdependent. Only when each member contributes, and is allowed to contribute, his or her own unique gifts will the body truly be whole and its ministry effective.

St Paul concludes the chapter by launching into his great hymn in praise of love – God's greatest gift because it is his own nature which he calls us to share in. So it is supremely by the way of love that any ordained priest will fulfil their distinctive and priestly ministry just as it is supremely by the way of love that the Christian community will fulfil its purpose to the world. To set forth the nature of the true and living God and to offer on behalf of the whole Universe the eucharistic response of worship, praise and thanksgiving.

On the nature of the Eucharist

The Eucharist has been central to the worship and spirituality of Christians since the very earliest days of the Church. In the Acts of the Apostles *'the breaking of the bread'* is part of the life of the community while as early as the time of St Paul this commemoration of the Lord's death is separated out from its original context within a shared meal and becomes a distinctive rite of worship. Inevitably there was discussion over the meaning of the rite and particularly over the interpretation of the words of Jesus, 'this is my body….this is my blood' – were they to be taken literally or figuratively?

In the Middle Ages an important factor was the philosophical language used. Neo-Platonism had been the dominant movement of thought in the Roman world when Christians first sought a philosophical expression of their teachings and it remained dominant until Aristotle's works, previously lost to the West, were translated from the Arabic in the twelfth century. It was St Albert the Great and St Thomas Aquinas who reformulated Christian doctrine in the context of Aristotelian Philosophy and for the Eucharist that meant that Jesus' words at the last supper were to be taken literally – the bread and wine of the Eucharistic action were nothing less than the actual flesh and blood of the Saviour. The Fourth Lateran Council of 1215 declared the doctrine of Transubstantiation which enshrines this interpretation of the manner of Christ's presence in the Eucharist. The feast of Corpus Christi was also introduced to celebrate this new teaching and it quickly established itself as one of the chief festivals of the year. If you think that makes it an innovation, the feast of Trinity Sunday wasn't to be introduced for another century!

Through all this though we should remember that the essential teaching of the Church is that Christ is truly present in every Eucharist – the doctrine of the Real Presence. Transubstantiation is a philosophical explanation of how our Lord is present. If you are not an Aristotelian then the language of transubstantiation will not be particularly helpful to you, but you can still believe fervently in the Real Presence without insisting on knowing 'how' our Lord is present.

When it comes to the sixteenth century the reformation divides the western Church and one of the chief areas of difference was of course over the understanding of the Eucharist – the Sacramental Body of Christ. The debate was in large part influenced by the revival of Platonic philosophy. Martin Luther was an Augustinian Canon and a student of the thought of St Augustine who was himself a Platonist. The Augustinians were the intellectual rivals of the Dominican friars, and St Thomas Aquinas was a Dominican. So one can describe the reformation as an intellectual debate – or struggle – as much as between Aristotelians and Platonists and between Dominicans and Augustinians as between Catholics and Protestants. Martin Luther never swerved from his belief in the Real Presence but it may well be that Archbishop Cranmer in England came to agree with some extreme Protestants who went so far as to deny the Real Presence.

But the twentieth century has seen considerable success in bridging some of these gaps The Anglican-Roman Catholic International Commission's agreed statements is particularly clear, even poetic, as when it says:

> In the Eucharistic celebration we anticipate the joys of the age to come. By the transforming action of the Spirit of God, earthly bread and wine become the heavenly manna and the new wine, the eschatological banquet for the new man: elements of the first creation become pledges and first fruits of the new heaven and the new earth.

Where Roman, Anglican and Protestant theologians are in such agreement then surely the Holy Spirit must have a hand in it somewhere! As well as, or indeed perhaps because of, this coming together of understanding the twentieth century also witnessed a shift in Eucharistic emphasis. Once again there is a clearer stress on the context of the fellowship meal and our gaze is not exclusively directed to the heavens or to the Host but also to our neighbour. The Eucharist has taken on a social dimension as well as its character as an act of objective devotion. This reminds us that Corpus Christi not only means the sacramental Body of Christ on the altar but also the mystical body of Christ which is the community of the Church. The sacramental Body is the mode of Christ's presence in the Church, the Church itself is the mode of Christ's presence in the world.

On the Liturgy of the Eucharist

Kyrie

Kyrie eleison, Lord, have mercy. All religion could perhaps be described as the attempt to make sense of human experience in its mixture of joy and sorrow, good and evil, light and dark. Christianity is that indeed, but it is also not so much our search for God and meaning as his search for us in order to give us meaning. In the Book of Genesis, 'God called to the man and said to him, Where art thou?' That is the heart of religion. The Bible is our record of God's revelation of himself to humanity and of humanity's response to that revelation. There is thus a fundamental continuity of divine purpose between the Old and New Testaments as we trace the story of God's unceasing work to draw sinful humanity back to himself. If there is much to be thankful for in this world, there is also much for which to be penitent. Karl Barth says that all creation is a cry for mercy. Our starting point must always be a vision of the holiness, love and power of God and in the light of this there will be a sense of our sin and of our unworthiness. *Lord have mercy.* But out of this will come God's free gift of forgiveness and a renewed sense of vocation as his son or daughter in the world.

Gloria

In C.S.Lewis' unusual and theological trilogy of science fiction, Lewis calls Earth the silent planet. He argues that all God's creation exists to give praise to the creator, but no praise reaches the heavens from the silent planet because sin has turned humanity from praise of God to self-centeredness. This accords well with one of St Augustine's definitions of sin which, he says, makes one *'incurvatus in se'* –

The problem with the silent planet is to be found in us of course. Nature in itself is not sinful – the animal world is not self-conscious and therefore does not make moral choices between good and evil. But humanity is at the apex of the natural world and in us the praise which all the natural world makes to its creator should become at last chosen, conscious and articulate. *Gloria in excelsis Deo – Glory to God in the Highest.* But whereas the natural world can only be natural we are never merely natural – we either rise above the natural to the supernatural or we fall beneath to the unnatural. This is our glory, and our doom.

To the Christian, the human is of course *homo sapiens*, but also *homo adorans* – it is in the nature of the beast to worship and give glory to God and, as a priest of creation, to give voice to the worship of the whole creation. By praising God we are doing that for which we were created and fulfilling our deepest purpose in life. To quote from Peter Shaffer's play Equus:

'either you worship or you shrink; it's as brutal as that!'

Credo

Credo in unum Deum – I believe in one God. Or should it be, we believe? Christianity is neither wholly individualistic nor entirely corporate in its assessment of the human condition. We are, as Christians, a body – the body of Christ. As Dietrich Bonhoeffer puts it, Christ existing as community. Another German theologian, Jurgen Moltmann, describes that community as 'a community of memory and hope.' Our memory is represented by the scriptures and the tradition contained in the great creeds of the Church. All summarise what God has done for us – the mighty works of God by which he has acted to save his people.

But if we look back to events of ultimate significance in the past we also need to look forward to their fulfilment in a future where history finds its consummation, for we are a community of hope as well as of memory. The Nicene Creed itself leads us from retrospect to prospect:

And I believe one holy catholic and apostolic Church. I acknowledge one baptism for the remission of sins. And I look for the resurrection of the dead, And the life of the world to come.

Sanctus

Something of the vision of God is surely found in beauty. Music, drama, literature, philosophy for some, a sense of history for me......beauty makes us stop being heedless of the meaning of life and has something about it of the eternal, something of God. But the Christian religion is more than a sense of the numinous, a sense of beauty. The vision at the heart of the Judaeo-Christian tradition is not aesthetic but ascetic; it is a moral vision of God's goodness and the good life to which he calls us.

Isaiah chapter 6 sums up for me the essential characteristics of the spiritual life because it points up that movement from vision to a sense of unworthiness, to the experience of forgiveness and, finally, a sense of vocation. Vision is foundational and, as the Book of Proverbs puts it, 'where there is no vision the people will perish.'

So what has been your moment of vision, when God has become real and personal rather than someone believed in because of the testimony of others? What has led you to the vision of God and prompted penitence, forgiveness and a sense of vocation?

Benedictus

To cry *'Benedictus, blessed is he who comes in the name of the Lord'* as we do in the Eucharist, is to join the crowds in Jerusalem when Jesus entered the city, and they were not welcoming him as a teacher but as the Messiah. There had been no king of David's line since the fall of the kingdom of Judah in 586BC yet the hope of an Anointed One, a Messiah, a king like David remained very much alive.

The Gospels make it very clear that it was only with difficulty the disciples of Jesus came to recognise him as Messiah because he was not what was expected – he was not obviously royal, was certainly unwarlike and never encouraged resistance to the Roman occupation of Judaea.

To understand the work of Jesus more deeply therefore we have to turn from the prophetic tradition of the Old Testament to the priestly tradition. Both prophet and priest saw that sin placed a barrier between God and man. For the prophet the remedy was repentance but for the priest more had to be done – atonement had to be made, and made by sacrifice. In other words something must be offered to God to make up for what had not been given in terms of moral obedience.

So Jesus, challenging the expectations of the time, offers us the suffering Messiah, drawing on the insights of the prophet we call Second Isaiah which showed that suffering, undeserved and willingly embraced, is redemptive of evil. Jesus is Lord and is the promised King of David's line. It is in him the Father fulfils the promised covenant but this fulfilment is found not in political or military power but in the sacrificial offering of his life in death by which he makes atonement for sin, reconciling God and man, and opening the Kingdom of Heaven to all united with him.

Agnus Dei

As we come to say '*O Lamb of God, who takes away the sin of the world*' we are reminded of the prophetic insight that the moral nature of our relationship to God demands repentance for our participation in sin. But also the serious nature of that sin demands that we cannot simply repent and forget – the priestly insight into the need for atonement is also required here.

The most consistent imagery for the mystery of Jesus' death in the liturgy of Holy Week is the main redemptive event of the Old Covenant, the Exodus. While the timing of the Gospels is different, all agree that the events of the Passion are to be understood in terms of a new Passover. At the last supper Jesus shares with his disciples bread and wine, with the astounding words '*this is my body, this is my blood.*' So Jesus interprets his own death as a new Passover for the new covenant. He is the Paschal Lamb, the Agnus Dei.

By this same act Jesus transformed the Jewish Passover meal into a rite by which his followers could for ever after share in the mystery of his passage through death to eternal life – his Exodus. By sharing in the Eucharistic meal, recalling his death and resurrection, Christians participate in these saving events. The cross reveals what was always true about God, his self-giving nature, and he gives us the privilege of sharing this most profound principle by which the world is sustained Eucharist by Eucharist, day by day, week by week.

On the Testaments

When we look at the Old Testament it is tempting to follow it through literally and to see it as first the Torah or Jewish Law, supposedly given to Moses in about 1,200 BC, then the histories of the kings up to the time of the prophets, and then the writings of the prophets from 750 to 550 BC, commenting on the people's failure to keep the Law. But scholars tell us that while some elements of the Torah may go back to Moses, like the Ten Commandments, most of it was written later and in response to the teaching of the prophets. The Law then enshrines the profound insights of the prophets and seeks to give them binding authority by placing them in the mouth of Moses.

The Old Testament is a vast collection of literature which has been brought together by different schools of editors who have sought to give the material cohesion and unity. The scholars who edited this literature were the heirs of the prophets and it is the insights of those prophets which give the Old Testament its essential unity. And the message of the prophets is that God has made known how he wants men and women to live; when they live according to his will he will extend his blessing upon them, but when they reject his law he will punish them. Even so, the hope of final blessing, for Israel at least, has the last word in the promise of a messianic deliverer and an age of blessedness in the future.

Without this theological background it would have been very difficult for the followers of Jesus to formulate an interpretation of his significance and achievement. And the New Testament is just that – an interpretation of the significance and achievement of Jesus. As with the Old Testament, it can look at first as if the New Testament presents first the facts of the life of Jesus, then the story of his followers and finally a set of letters by some of those followers expounding their interpretation of the Gospels. But in fact most of the letters were written first and the Gospels reflect the interpretation of

Jesus already formulated by St Paul in his epistles. The Gospels are not objective narratives but express the understanding of Jesus already prevalent in the communities among which they were written.

2. Exegesis: the liturgical year

Advent

Beginnings and Endings

Half a year has gone by since we came to the end of the great cycle of the Church's festivals with Corpus Christi and Pentecost; today we begin the cycle again with the season of Advent which leads us to Christmas. This then is the beginning of the year; but it is also, strangely, the end and climax of the year. For Advent not only points us backward to that historical event at Bethlehem and to the beginning of the drama of Jesus Christ, it also points forward to an event that transcends history, to what has been called the Last Day, when the drama of Jesus Christ and the drama of this universe will be brought to their glorious consummation. If Advent means coming, we have to look not only at the historical coming of Jesus as the child of Mary but also at what is called his Second Coming in glory and judgement. I want therefore to look at these two different dimensions to the Advent season - the historical birth of Jesus and the belief that Jesus is at the same time the one in whom all history finds its meaning and end.

The coming of the Kingdom of God

In the creed we regularly declare our belief that Jesus will come again to judge the quick and the dead, but we tend to defer the idea of judgement, putting it off as something that will happen at some point after death. But judgement is not so much something that happens in the future, but rather something that happens all the time. In St John's Gospel, Jesus says 'this is the judgement, that the light has come into the world, and men loved darkness rather than the light because their deeds were evil.' So in our heart of hearts we know we judge ourselves daily by the choices we make; one way or another we all choose between light and darkness, good and evil, love and selfishness. Day by day these may well seem very small choices of no great significance, but by these choices we build up our personal histories and we choose which side we shall take at the end of the day. Ultimately we build up or diminish by these apparently insignificant choices our moral courage and strength, opting time and again for what I have called before either 'strenuous liberty' or 'bondage with ease'.

Daniel's great vision of the time of great conflict sees God's righteous people suffer for a time but triumph in the end. Although Daniel wrote in the form of a vision, he was in fact describing the troubles his people were experiencing in their day, and he wrote to encourage them with the promise of an eternal reward. But he did something else as well, he made them see that the little choices they were faced with day by day were actually part of a cosmic warfare of good and evil. Every moral choice matters not, perhaps, because of its immediate consequences but because it is part of a much bigger issue being fought out in the whole universe: will God's creation incline towards his ways of love and goodness, finding its proper fulfilment in the Kingdom of Jesus Christ, or will it ever more and more turn away from God towards selfishness and so disintegration. You and I daily make choices that are part of this cosmic drama.

The Jews at the time of Jesus were full of these prophecies of Daniel and were consequently on the look-out for signs that God would intervene in history and so vindicate his chosen people. The message of Jesus was to cut through all this – present realities were more important than future ideas of righteousness or reign. When he speaks of the signs of the end he adds 'truly, I say to you, this generation will not pass away before all these things take place'. In other words, once again he is saying that judgement is not something that can be relegated to a distant future, it is something that happens day by day in every choice we make for or against his way of self-giving love. And if judgement is not so much a future as a present reality, then so is the kingdom of God itself. In St Luke's Gospel when the Pharisees actually ask Jesus when the kingdom of God is to come he replies, '*the kingdom of God is not coming with signs to be observed, nor will they say: Lo, here it is! Or, there! For behold, the kingdom of God is in the midst of you*'. Now sometimes that phrase has been translated to mean that the kingdom is an interior spiritual thing within us, but I think it more faithful to the Gospel to understand it to mean that God's kingdom is known in how we share our lives with each other. The kingdom of God is among us, in the choices we make each day, in how we treat each other.

We are not so at home now with the language of Daniel's vision, nor with the imagery of St John's Revelation, but they use the vivid imagery of cosmic warfare to bring home to their readers the vast stage on which the drama of human living is set. We may try and reduce the backdrop or push some aspects of the drama into the future so that the choices we face do not seem so very serious. But actually that option is not open to us. The very faculties that make us human and raise us above the instinctual life of the animals demand that we take our proper place in the universe and shoulder the great responsibility of all that it means to be human. For it means to be a co-worker with God in the building of the earth and in bringing the whole creation to its fulfilment in obedience to Christ.

Season of the Prophets

There are prophets even today. You know my fascination with the writings of Laurens Van Der Post, Carl Gustav Jung and Hans Kung. Some journalists too have the prophetic touch – high on my list would be Connor Cruise O'Brien. But what is this prophecy that is so much a part of the Advent liturgy? Well, Biblical prophecy is not predicting the future – Amos is no Hebrew Nostradamos! Hebrew prophets were rather like the best kind of journalist: closely in touch with world affairs, with the mood of the nation, with the hopes and fears of ordinary people and with the ambitions, abilities and weaknesses of national leaders. Unlike any journalist I know, however, the prophets of Israel were first and foremost theologians. They interpreted history as the context of God's purposes for men and women – seeing God not as a remote creator withdrawn from the affairs of the world but as an active participant in the lives of individuals and of nations.

When the northern Kingdom of Israel was overrun by the Assyrians the disciples of Amos and Hosea fled south to Jerusalem, taking with them a particular prophetic critique of society. There they joined forces with the prophetic movement of Judah comprising the followers of Isaiah and together they provoked a religious revolution.. And the first great editorial work on what was to become the Hebrew Bible was done by these disciples of the prophets. They assembled the legends of the patriarchs, Moses and Joshua, the story of the conquest of Canaan of the first Kings and Israel and they cast the whole into a single continuous drama of salvation.

History was thus given a theological interpretation that enabled the Jews to understand and survive the experience of the destruction of Jerusalem and the temple and the seventy years of exile in Babylon. To quote one theologian, *'the Jews went into exile a nation and came out a religion'*, but it was a religion with a profound and prophetic theology that remains central to Christian thought as well.

Let me mention just two essential elements. First, history is interpreted as linear whereas in the ancient world it was seen as circular. History therefore has a beginning and an end – it's going somewhere and it has a purpose. So how we live matters – matters to us, matters to God, matters to our eternal destiny. God cares for us, we are important to him, he watches over us. And there is something God wants from us, that we should grow up into true human maturity - which in later Christian thought will be called 'the measure of the stature of the fullness of Christ.' When we turn away from this life that God intends, choosing instead something smaller, selfish or ignoble, then God is grieved and pained: the prophets would have said 'angered'.

This could lead to an impasse where a diminished humanity confronts an angry God. But look at the second essential strand of prophetic theology. Beyond God's anger, his grief and his pain there is his love; beyond his judgement there is his forgiveness; beyond punishment there is restoration. The prophecies of Isaiah and Jeremiah and Ezekiel look forward to a new age of justice when God and humanity will live in harmony and the entire creation find its fulfilment. Meanwhile, here in the midst of history, we have a life to live, a law to guide us, a call to respond to and one true God to worship.

Faithfulness and Sanctification

Zechariah, Simeon, Anna, Mary, Joseph, James and John, Andrew and Peter, Saul of Tarsus, Nicodemos: all faithfully waited in their own way and in their own time for God to act and all in a way were remarkably unprepared when God did act. Perhaps they had grown over-accustomed to waiting, perhaps they had come to a point where they no longer genuinely expected to witness the mighty works of God. All however had their lives turned upside-down and none could go back to the ways things were for them beforehand.

I want to draw, very briefly, some conclusions for our own lives from these figures in the scriptures. The starting point for them all is faithfulness to God within their own religious experience and tradition, and they not only witness to the ways God has already acted in the past they also wait for his new action in the present and the future. But for all of them the manner of God's new action comes as a surprise and as a demand of more than they might have thought possible. God, you see, always calls us to grow into greater stature than we had thought was ours. In the language of Christian spirituality, we move from the life of faithfulness to the life of sanctification. But such theological words disguise the down-to-earth reality of what it is like when God acts. Perhaps the trouble is that we expect God to act in ways easily described in traditional religious language: in fact, he acts in earthy, human ways, demanding of us not the superhuman but the more intense commitment to human qualities already existent within us.

Where the Holy Spirit is active everything changes and we see the world and its possibilities in a new light. Pasolini's interpretation of the effects of the coming of the Holy Spirit in his film 'Theorum' was very controversial, but it did make one point very powerfully – that there is no going back. God's action in our lives cannot be undone, things can never be the same again. The Christian vision of life points us through faithfulness to openness to the Holy Spirit who always calls us further than we expected to travel, who reveals to us potential we had never dreamed of, stretching us to new dimensions of humanity we had thought impossible. The scriptures never suggest response to the Holy Spirit is easy but what they do promise is that God himself is faithful. They only demand what we can truly obtain and so fulfil in us his eternal longing that we may grow up, as St Paul says, into the fullness of the stature of the person of Christ.

Christmas

The holly bears a prickle

Of all the names associated with Jesus - *Messiah, Saviour, Redeemer, Second Adam, Wonderful Counsellor, Prince of Peace* – I like especially *Emmanuel,* which means *God with us* and comes from a prophecy quoted in St Matthew's Gospel. After all, God could be very distant, like the sort of God a physicist like Stephen Hawking might just propose, playing dice with the universe: God could exist and could have made this vast universe, and not really care about us, our doings, our destiny. But whatever else is hidden in the mystery of the birth of Jesus, we find this sense of a God who is with us, close to us, caring for us. We discover a sense of a God who made us out of love to be at one with him forever. A God moreover who responds to the distancing of ourselves from him by not over-riding his precious gift of freedom, not forcing us, but by inviting us back, in T.S.Eliot's words in The Four Quartets, *'with the drawing of this Love and the voice of this Calling.'*

This loving-caring is shown to us at Bethlehem as it is shown to us also at Calvary – it is revealed to us at the crib as well as at the cross. And it is not revealed as doctrine but as experience – and so revealed perhaps with that same potential mixture of faith and doubt, understanding and mystery that might characterise our own believing and celebrating this and every Christmas. Think of Joseph's confusion, love and doubt; Mary pondering mystery in her heart; and shepherds simply gazing at a new-born child. And the Magi? Eliot, in his poem, *The Journey of the Magi,* has one of the Wise Men express the same search for understanding in the face of experience and mystery:

Were we led all that way for Birth or death? There was a birth, certainly, We had evidence and no doubt. I had seen birth and death, But had thought they were different; this Birth was Hard and bitter agony for us, like Death, our death.

For me, one of the very reassuring things about Christmas is that, if our ears and hearts and minds are open, simply singing carols is a powerful re-telling of the Christian story. Modern carols tend towards the sugary and sentimental but medieval carols especially do not shrink from reminding us exactly who this child is and what he will accomplish for humanity. *O come all ye faithful* quotes the Nicene creed, *The Holly and the Ivy* points to the passion by referring to blood, thorn and gall and *We three kings* expounds the meaning of the gifts and myrrh with 'its bitter perfume breathes a life of gathering doom; sorrowing, sighing, bleeding, dying, sealed in the stone-cold tomb.'

Even in the midst of celebrating Jesus' birth we are not allowed to forget that the reason for his birth is the redemption of the world by his innocent suffering and death. If our celebrations seem tawdry and superficial – far too much indulgence, eating and drinking while half the world is starving – the Christmas festival is saved by retaining this deeply theological stratum. It may go unnoticed by many, even most. But I am sure these profound reflections in some of our most popular carols will ultimately touch the hearts of many and remind us all that today we celebrate not simply a birth but the renewal of the whole of creation and the restoration of unity with God for ever.

The Word was made flesh

I think a lot of people find it strange that carol services often begin with the story of Adam and Eve in the Garden of Eden, but we have to understand that something is wrong with humanity if we are to make sense of what God does to put it right. Through the long ages that science describes as the evolution of the universe and human life, the Creator was calling into being creatures capable of knowing him and enjoying a relationship with him. But a real relationship – now as then – depends on the recognition of the way things really are. Whatever we make of the ancient story of Eden, it is seeking to describe what is wrong about men and women and our relationship to the Creator. One way or another we all place ourselves at the centre of our own universe and so get everything out of proportion. And the inevitable result is what we see in today's world – war and violence, the ugly imbalance of wealth and poverty, and the myriad forms taken by man's inhumanity to man.

But this is not the destiny of God's creation! We were created that we might know God, love him and enjoy him for ever. And we must not think that God has somehow been taken by surprise at the way things have turned out. Perhaps it was inevitable. Certainly the scriptures make it clear that it was always God's plan from the beginning that he would enter without reserve into his creation to ensure the achievement of its destiny.

And quite simply that is what we celebrate today. That in this child in the manger at Bethlehem God himself takes flesh to live a human life and so consecrate our humanity and bring it to its goal. A French theologian and scientist, Teilhard de Chardin, spoke of the incarnation as God pouring a *phylum d'amour* – a test-tube of love – into the experiment of his human creation. And that is just what the experiment needed to turn humanity from destructive self-centeredness into the ways of self-sacrifice and generosity.

One carol rather gloomily tells us that 'beneath the angel-strain have rolled two thousand years of wrong', which suggests that the incarnation was unsuccessful in changing humanity. Certainly there is still so much that is wrong with the way we live and the ways of the world, but I remain confident that the Christian experiment will accomplish the task set us – which is to be leaven in the world and to bring light in dark places. The incarnation is not simply an event in the past, something limited to first century Galilee and Judaea. John Betjeman wrote famously that '*God was Man in Palestine and lives today in Bread and Wine.*' So the incarnation lives on in the community of Christ's disciples, nourished as we are by the sharing of this mystical bread and wine. So in a quite astounding way the destiny of God and of his creation, and the fulfilment of the purpose of the incarnation, is literally and metaphorically in our hands.

The yes of the Son knew the yes of the maid

By God's redemption we see the difference between slavery and freedom, sinfulness and holiness; and the redeeming works of God we celebrate most particularly are marked by Christmas and Easter, Ascension and Pentecost. These are feasts of God's initiative.

But '*the yes of the Son knew the yes of the maid*'. These words from the lovely hymn sung by the sisters of West Malling remind us that the story of our redemption does not end with God's initiative – human response is also part of the story. We cannot make a final separation between the story of what God has done for humanity and the story of how humanity has responded to God. To celebrate Christmas is to rejoice both in the Son and in the mother, just as to celebrate Pentecost is to rejoice both in the gift of the Holy Spirit and in the Apostles. Saints days and the festivals of Our Lady, like the feasts of Our Lord, are also celebrations of our redemption.

A Kingdom present and to come

One of the theological phrases I have used a number of times over Christmas is that through the incarnation God ceases to be *wholly other* than man and women. Describing God as we so often do in terms of philosophical absolutes, it is said that God is entirely different from us – he does not have a body, he does not die, he is not limited in knowledge, space or time. But in the incarnation God does take to himself a human body and all the limitations of the human condition – he is no longer *wholly other.*

While the Church is not the same thing as the Kingdom of God it is a sign that points to the Kingdom and it does share some of the characteristics of the Kingdom. It may be an earthly institution at one level, encumbered by buildings and investments, hierarchies and disagreements. But at another level it exists as a spiritual community of men and women bearing witness to the God who is not *wholly other.*

To live as a member of the Church is to attempt to live already by the values of the Kingdom, even though we know there is always more to learn about God's will for us. The challenge is to incorporate the values of the Kingdom into the way we live day by day, while being open to an ever greater awareness of its nature and possibilities.

Ben Okri, the Nigerian poet, has written an epic poem embracing our hopes on the eve of a new millennium. I can't quote it all but part of the second stanza seems appropriate:

A quality of enlightenment
A sense of the limited time we have
Here on earth to live magnificently
To be as great and happy as we can
To explore our potential to the fullest
And to lose our fear of death
Having gained a greater love
And reverence for life
And its incommensurable golden brevity.

Epiphany

Today's feast – January 6th - is certainly the Church's original celebration of the birth of our Lord. The Orthodox churches of the East still keep the date while only the Western church felt the need to move the celebration to December 25th in order to take over the great annual romp in the city of Rome, the Saturnalia. Some might say that in the end it looks as if the pagan romp has taken over Christmas! All the more reason, therefore, for Christians to hold on to this more ancient feast.

How does God reveal himself to us?

Judaism, always so strictly monotheistic, traditionally saw God accompanied both by his Word and his Wisdom. And over time collections of anecdotes and sayings, often drawn from Egyptian and Mesopotamian traditions and often at variance with the theology of the Old Testament in general, began to be brought together and preserved in what is called wisdom literature – especially the books of Ecclesiastes and Proverbs in the Old Testament and Wisdom and Ecclesiasticus in the Apocrypha.

Wisdom was also important to Greek thinkers who called themselves philosophers, lovers of wisdom. Lacking a revelation of God in the manner of the Jews, Greek thinkers took as their starting point the material world and human experience. And of course Christianity owes much to Greek philosophical thought as well as to Judaism. The New Testament was written in Greek, its authors drawing on the vocabulary and concepts of Greek religion. By the time a developed Christian theology was being worked out at the great Christian councils of the 4th and 5th centuries, Greek philosophical ideas were also important. The greatest church in Christendom of the time, Hagia Sophia in Constantinople, was dedicated to Holy Wisdom.

Just as the Word of God was identified with the Son incarnate in Jesus so the Wisdom of God came to be identified with the Holy Spirit. Thus God relates to the world by his Word which he addresses through his prophets and in his Son, and also by his Wisdom which inspires men and women of every age, opening to them the mysteries of creation and of human experience which are themselves pointers to the nature and character of the Creator.

But speaking about knowledge of God in this way always opens up the problem of the difference between our general awareness of divine reality and the specifically Christian knowledge of God. Greek philosophers like Plato may have argued for the existence of an absolute Principle underlying all existence and all experience, but this is a very long way from the Christian belief in a loving Father who cares about us so much that he acts to draw us to himself through incarnation, crucifixion and resurrection. In the end all revelation of God and all human knowledge of God is subordinated to God's revelation of himself in Jesus. In Michael Ramsey's words, *'In God there is nothing that is not like Jesus'*. So for a New Year's resolution, read the Gospels, and then read them again.

The gleam that broke in

What the Epiphany story suggests for me is that these scholars, confronted by a new phenomenon which could not be solved by astrology, felt under genuine compulsion to abandon theory in favour of adventure. Those Wise Men did but follow the gleam that broke in upon their patient studies: they rose and followed the star. So often, just as we think we have it all worked out, a place for everything and everything in its place, then something new will enter our experience and challenge our presuppositions and our understanding. It is always an invitation to journey.

What we all have to learn eventually is that life is not a problem to be solved – rather it is a mystery to be entered, explored and enjoyed. Sooner or later we shall all have to leave behind the comfortable world of theory and construct and plunge into the harsher world of reality and challenge. Only when false securities are left behind shall we find ourselves free to journey to our Bethlehem – where for us the truth about who we are and where God dwells is discovered. At that point in our human experience there is only one possible response: like the Wise Men we must worship, opening our treasures and offering the deepest things of our lives: our gold, our incense, our myrrh.

Lent

Lord they believe; help thou their unbelief

In Christian theology there are two kinds of faith. Scholars speak of the *fides qua creditor* – the faith by which I believe – and the *fides quae creditor* – the faith which is believed. This is an important distinction. The first kind of faith is a broad gut instinct that life is essentially good rather than bad, to be affirmed rather than rejected, meaningful rather than not. This deep, underlying conviction of value in human life is, thankfully, widespread among the people I meet – young and old, rich and poor – though it is not, of course, universal.

But it is harder than ever for these men and women of faith to affirm the specifics of the Christian Gospel, not least because of modern astronomy, modern physics and modern history. Modern astronomy marks the end of anthropocentricity – we can no longer believe that humanity on this planet lies at the heart and centre of the universe. Modern physics presents a universe vast in time as well as in space and it is hard to assert that the universe exists, all 15 billion years of it, simply in order that the human race may flourish, though this is the Christian claim. Finally modern history. The previous understanding of history as an inevitable and divinely ordained progression towards a fully Christian society – democratic, tolerant, prosperous, scientific, humane – came to an end with the trench warfare of the first World War, the Armenian massacres in Turkey, the camps of Nazi Germany. No longer can we speak of providence in the same way.

So much of the language the Church uses is borrowed from earlier societies with their own religious world view and it will not serve the proclamation of the Gospel to those who simply have no religious world view at all. The ideas with which theologians of earlier centuries defended Christianity in controversy with Jewish theologians or Greek philosophers will simply have no impact today.

With Paul Tillich we might want to affirm that the purpose of creation is that *'a place was provided in which life could grow and history develop, in which words could be heard and love be felt, and in which truth could be discovered and the Eternal adored.'* But how then can we articulate salvation meaningfully?

New directions

Lawrence Goring once commented that 'art brings us to the edge of theophany', but art, like theology, has had to evolve. I think I had got as far as to recognise that after the development of photography art could no longer be merely representational – it had to look to express an inwardness usually hidden from the camera. But Charles Pickstone, in a Sion College lecture I heard recently, pointed not so much to photography as to Freud and Einstein to explain the new direction in art taken at the beginning of the twentieth century – Surrealism and Cubism. Freud revealed the depth and disorder of the unconscious mind while Einstein revealed the relativity of all things in place of their previously presumed stability. The work of these two men signalled the end of the world of renaissance humanism which had enjoyed an Indian summer in the Victorian and Edwardian eras. The triumph of reason, celebrated in the accepted canons of art and culture, was shattered by the guns of the Somme and the holocaust of Nazi Germany.

Similarly I want to suggest that it is no longer any use interpreting Jesus' death in terms that are no longer meaningful. In the world of late Antiquity in which Christianity became the established religion of the Roman Empire, Christ was presented as the one who has overcome death and therefore who held out to humanity the possibility of eternal life. In the Middle Ages, Christ was the judge who could reward his faithful with heaven and save them from hell. But despite the radical changes that have swept the intellectual life of Europe since the Renaissance, the Church has not changed the essential language of its teaching. So the Church has slowly lost its sway over the minds and hearts of the people – first the intellectuals and more recently, since 1918, the general population.

But in spite of this we still see religion continuing to be a force in the affairs of the world. Christianity may be waning in England but grows stronger than ever in Africa while taking on ever greater political significance in South America and Eastern Europe. So I want to ask if there is a different way in which we can speak today of Christ our Saviour that will make sense in post Freudian and post Einsteinian world. Humanity's religious sense is clearly as real as ever; but what kind of theophany will be of relevance now?

When Pilate brings Jesus out to the people he says '*ecce homo*' – *behold the man*. But I like to interpret this as meaning *behold man – now at last you see man as God always intended him to be.* But how does this perfect man, so complete in his own life and experience, actually save you and me, and from what? Firstly I might want to say that evil can be defined as anything which works against my development into the fully mature person I have the potential to be. Past ideals of humanity have often been couched in the language of purity but I would prefer to utilise terms of maturity. Purity suggests someone who has held back and avoided the risk of plunging into the maelstrom of human experience. The mature person on the other hand has certainly acted – and made mistakes – but has come through the experiences of the world enriched, deepened, softened, made wise, loving and forgiving. Secondly if Jesus were only a man then he would at most be an example, what Carl Gustav Jung calls '*the supreme expression of the anthropos for western man.*' But because Jesus is fully God as well as fully man, as Christian orthodoxy insists, then his victory is ours as well. Paul develops the understanding of Christ as a Cosmic Person incorporating all humanity into himself. Evil did its worst at Calvary but its worst was not as powerful as the will of God for life and love for all. So God's victory at Calvary is also humanity's triumph. A defeated enemy fights fierce and fights dirty but we know we need not fear. We are saved, because this power of evil was overcome once and for all in the darkness of a Friday afternoon outside Jerusalem.

Falling upwards

Something went wrong with my planning this year. I usually manage to preach on the creation and avoid this week's theme of the fall. You see, I put great emphasis on the words from Genesis at the end of the six days of creation – *God saw all that he had made, and behold it was very good.* Original goodness – now that I do believe! But what of original sin?

As so often, it is to St Augustine that we owe these theological ideas. He naturally believed that Adam and Eve were the parents of the whole human race and he taught that their first transgression in the Garden of Eden were passed on to all their descendants who are born as a result of the tainted act of procreation. Now, on the whole, western Christians no longer believe this. To us the theory of evolution, if not proven, is still the most plausible explanation of the origin of the species. And we need not feel that this biology contradicts the theology of the Bible. But you can see the theological problem that this creates: if sin is not passed from generation to generation, does each one of us begin life in the innocence we associate with Adam and Eve in the story of Genesis? Well, no, we don't! Because, of course, we are born into the human race with its long history. And if Carl Gustav Jung is to be believed, then we each inherit psychologically, if not theologically, the history of the human race in what he calls the Collective Unconscious.

Babies can be wilful and utterly self-centered, but what might be called sinful as the conscious act of an adult cannot be called that when it is the action of a child too young to make conscious moral choices. And when parents realise that children have developed to that point at which they can make conscious moral choices there may be a touch of sadness when it is realised that innocence is being left behind, but they cannot regret this development – it is an essential part of growth into full and mature humanity. Nor can the creator be sorry when we leave behind an animal-like innocence and come to the point when we can begin to achieve the potential he gave us to more fully bear his image. As Archbishop William Temple remarked, 'if there is a fall, it is a fall upwards.'

In a recent Lily Montagu lecture the Chief Rabbi located the source of what goes wrong in human experience in the realm of our relationships – since Genesis says that everything in the creation is good until the phrase *it is not good for man to be alone.* And that leads very quickly to conflict between Adam and Eve, and fratricidal strife between Cain and Abel. Well, we do not know how we might be in complete isolation – we only exist in relationships, in communities, in families. It is in these contexts that issues of self-centeredness come to the fore but it is also in these contexts that we have the possibility of transcending instinctual drives of self-interest. Surely, if we ask what is meant by being made in the image of God, it is not only in our capacity for free moral choice but also in our potential for entering into relationships which share the nature of divine, self-giving love.

So, I think we need a new theological model for the human story. It isn't simply a drama in three acts: innocence, fall, redemption. We need rather to think of a single continuous unfolding of the divine purpose. Here, created with enormous potential for good or ill, we wrestle with the human condition – peak experiences as well as times of despond, the hopes and fears, opportunities lost as well as new beginnings made. It is through all these we make our pilgrimage towards the City of God, and maybe we have sometimes to look back along the path we have trodden to find that we can be grateful even for the bad times because they are part of the way we have been awakened to our truest nature as children of God and citizens of his kingdom.

The measure of all things

When Renaissance thought rejected the medieval Christian model of Judgement it came up with an alternative, a model they called *Uomo Universale* or Universal Man. What came to be known as renaissance man, a model of physical beauty, strength, one who was a courtier, a musician, an artist, a scientist – all rolled into one. Since most or all fell short of the ideal they found themselves judged by it. The Renaissance was the springtime of humanism and similar ideals were continued by the rationalism of the Eighteenth and liberalism of the Nineteenth centuries. But our age, post modern and more cynical, while also rejecting the Christian model does not even pick up the humanist alternative. Not 'Man' but every man is now the measure of all things.

In such a permissive society, without moral guilt and judgement, people can look with amazement or confusion or criticism at a Church which retains a high moral demand. And that high moral demand is not contained in a code or set of commandments but in the person of Jesus. Not only is he Son of God but also the model of our Christian living - for our religion is more than believing in Jesus, it involves following his example. By this are we judged – and of course we fall short but we are ever held by forgiveness. To be judged and forgiven in the Christian community with its high ideal of human living is far more meaningful than to live without ideal, without judgement and without forgiveness in isolation, however splendid that isolation might superficially seem. This is to reduce human life to the satisfaction of appetite and desire which leads ultimately to despair. Mature human living begins when we can look beyond these things and beyond ourselves – when we cease to be the measure of all things.

As St Paul wrote, *'I beg you to lead a life worthy of the calling to which you have been called.....until we attain to mature manhood, to the measure of the stature of the fullness of Christ.'*

Passiontide

The death of the Lord

As we follow the drama of the Lord's death each Passiontide we encounter a great deal of anger and violence, suspicion and cruelty, cowardice and shame. I wonder if this is not unique in the literature of the world's great religions. Here at the very core of our religious observance we are not faced by tranquillity, a calm spirituality or a mood of quiet contemplation. No, we are in the world of action and power politics. Here are scheming clerics, bullying soldiers, a notorious harlot, a vacillating provincial governor, a convicted terrorist and followers who seem little better than fair-weather friends, one a betrayer. The crowd scenes could be on almost any edition of the news today.

There is no escapism here, this is the stuff of reality. And perhaps the only real stranger in this drama is Jesus himself in his strange passivity as he allows himself to be handed over to the violence of the guard, the casuistry of the High Priest, the failure of Roman justice, the whim of the crowds. Jesus is passive because he has surrendered himself to the will of his Father and he sees events rushing to their determined end. When he was still at Bethany, in comparative safety, and Mary anointed him with the costly ointment, Jesus interprets her action as a part of this inevitable progress to his death – his body anointed for burial. It is a moment of great beauty and pathos, a moment of stillness amid events hastening to their end.

There will be many opportunities for us to make a not dissimilar offering in the days to come. The vehicle of the liturgy will offer us the chance to show sympathy and compassion with the Lord, will offer moments of beauty and pathos and opportunities for us to offer the most precious gift we have. But the Christian tradition would never let us rest with a religion that was merely liturgical – as if we were somehow detached from events and politics and social responsibility. We must show sympathy and compassion not just symbolically in church but actively in the world – or else what we do in church becomes mere outward show. What we do for Jesus in symbol and ceremony, we must surely do for those who are even today broken, unjustly imprisoned, abandoned or mistreated. For the drama of Calvary is enacted constantly in our own cities, our own society, our own lives.

Following the way of the cross we will find we are not merely spectators of an epic drama of events long ago, rather we are participating in the central mystery of human life. He whose life is eternal identified himself with our humanity without reserve and accepted human death that we might in turn identify ourselves with him and so share his risen and eternal life. And how do we identify with him? In baptism, yes, and in the eucharist, and also in serving the poor and needy even as he served us in our great poverty and need, so that at the last we may all share in the joys of his kingdom.

The Meaning of his Death

As we read the narrative of the Lord's death it is possible to be left feeling that things all went wrong after Jesus' triumphant and joyful entry into the city that we mark on Palm Sunday. But things didn't go wrong – it is the divine purpose that Jesus should fulfil the deep mystery of his messiahship by dying on the cross. But we may well ask why? The answer for me is that the purpose of the incarnation is not that the Son should come to teach us the truth as if that is all that is needed to put right our relationship with the Father. It is not that we are ignorant and do not know how we should live but rather that we are rebellious and refuse to live the way we have been taught by Moses and the prophets. Jesus' essential work is not to teach but to redeem.

To put the biblical case we have to employ the language of Genesis. Men and women were created in the image of God, which I understand to mean that, like God himself, we have moral freedom: we can choose freely to do good or we can choose equally freely to do evil. Not all choices are obviously good or evil but which of us can say we have never, knowingly and freely, chosen to do what we know to be wrong? In the mythological language of Genesis there were two very special trees in the garden of Eden, the tree of the knowledge of good and evil and the tree of life. Adam and Eve were forbidden the first but could eat freely of the second. Choosing knowledge however, they were driven from the garden and deprived of the fruit of the tree of life – and so faced death. The serpent, however, was not lying in telling Adam and Eve that when they ate of the fruit of the first tree that their eyes would be opened and they would be like God, knowing good and evil. While we may continue to be aware of the negative consequences that can accompany humanity's advancement in knowledge, we cannot regret that choice of knowledge over ignorance.

St Paul calls Jesus a second Adam. In him humanity is given a second chance, and in another garden another choice is made – not to take away the knowledge of good and evil but to enable us to direct that knowledge aright. In the life and death of Jesus the will of God is at last fulfilled – humanity has obeyed God and kept the divine law, for in that mystery that we call the sacramental principle because it has been done in him it has been done in all humanity. The innocent Jesus dies the death of disobedient humanity and is vindicated in resurrection and indeed we cannot make sense of the death of Jesus except in terms of the resurrection. And the evidence that Jesus' death is not the end of the story, apart from the evidence of Scripture, is our presence in church and the millions of Christians observing this solemn season. We come together not to mourn but to mark this stage on the shared journey that takes us on to the feast of the Resurrection, to Ascension and Pentecost.

This story is no tragedy – nor indeed a comedy. It is history. The history of what God has done by his incarnation in Jesus in whom he has drawn close to us. And if in response we would draw close to God, it is in Jesus that we have found this to be possible. For we have become members of his mystical body, the Church, and, empowered by the Spirit and proclaiming the resurrection, in us and through us the work of the incarnation goes forward.

Easter

Christus Vincit : Christus Regnat: Christus Imperat

The site in Jerusalem of Calvary and Christ's tomb is contained within one of the greatest shrines of Christendom, the church we call the Holy Sepulchre but which Orthodox Christians call the Anastasis – the Church of the Resurrection.

I believe these names are very significant. Enter most churches in the Latin West and you will find they are very often dominated by the symbol of the death of Our Lord – the crucifix on the altar, the rood screen, the stations of the cross. And while many Protestant churches lack this kind of visual symbolism, nevertheless I believe that most Protestant theology has been dominated by the death of the Lord.

But enter a church in the Greek or Russian East and you will always find the interior dominated by the representation of the Risen Lord – the *Pantocrator* or Ruler of All. There may be all sorts of reasons why this is so, not least because Christianity in the West was shaped during a time of imperial collapse and barbarian invasion and later was enormously influenced by the sufferings of the black death. Either way I do not want to banish the symbol of the dying Lord – heaven knows there are so many times when the symbol of divine suffering is what we can best identify with and what we most desperately need to know. But it is neither the whole story nor the last chapter of the story.

Before Calvary, Jesus might be seen as a figure limited to one century and to an obscure province of the Roman Empire. After the Resurrection Jesus transcends both history and geography, sums up the human condition – its struggle, its pain, its potential, its irrepressible longing – and confirms the victory over the limitations of life and of death. Jesus himself said prophetically, 'except a grain of wheat falls into the ground and dies, it remains alone. But if it dies it yields a rich harvest.' Jesus died and is risen – and we are his harvest. Alleluia.

The Areopagus

Have you ever been to Athens? If you have then I imagine you will have walked up the Sacred Way to the Acropolis. Half way up is the spot called the Hill of Mars where Paul addressed the people of Athens and told them about Jesus and the resurrection. Paul's hearers were most intrigued by his belief in the resurrection and wanted to know more of that - we read in St Luke that the Athenians loved nothing better than telling or hearing something new. Indeed it has been suggested that Christianity became the dominant religion of the Roman Empire a couple of hundred years later precisely because it was uniquely able to promise eternal life. But by the Middle Ages, when the idea of eternal life was no longer new, concern shifted to how exactly one might spend eternity – in heaven or hell – and that became the dominant thrust of the Church's mission and teaching. By the modern period the context had changed again. Away from the question of life after death, away from the issue of whether that life be in heaven or hell, to settle on the much more profound uncertainty about whether the life we lead in this present has any meaning or purpose in itself. We are a society, like it or not, with a profound existential doubt.

Paul, addressing his hearers on the Hill of Mars, was aware that one of their chief concerns was a longing for assurance about the future. In the religious marketplace of contemporary London we need to be sure that the Church is not providing answers to questions no longer being asked. Our celebration of Easter therefore is not just a rejoicing for a victory won long ago, nor is it just a celebration of the future promise of eternal life, it is just as much a reflection of the overwhelming exuberance of men and women who recognise that Jesus has demonstrated once and for all the value and meaning of the lives we live today.

The Community of the Resurrection

I feel I have grasped something recently about the nature of resurrection and the way it is recorded in the New Testament. What I feel struck by very powerfully is that in the resurrection narratives we are dealing with the transition from our Lord's individual existence in a physical body to the different form of his existence of which we are a part as members of his mystical body, the Church.

John Chapter 21 is a very important part of this. Now Peter's denial of Jesus is recorded in all four gospels but only John records Peter's restoration to his position as leader of the remaining eleven disciples when Jesus asks Peter three times if he loves him. Many of you will know that there is a dimension to this story which is completely missing in English and only obvious in Greek. Greek has three words for love: *philia* is brotherly love, *eros* is erotic love and *agape* is sacrificial love. First Jesus asks if Peter loves him with sacrificial love – *agape*. Peter replies that he loves Jesus with *philia* – brotherly love. A second time Jesus asks for the highest form of love and Peters offers back brotherly love. So the third time Jesus asks Peter if he has brotherly love for him. Peter is hurt because Jesus lowers his expectations of him and so finally he replies, *'Lord, you know everything. You know that I do feel for you that highest form of love that is truly sacrificial and akin to the love of God himself.'*

On each of these occasions Jesus charges Peter with the task of feeding and tending his sheep. What can this mean but what we call pastoral care. Here are the very beginnings of the Church – a community of men and women who believe in the resurrection of the Lord and who share the quality of sacrificial love which was central to Jesus' own life. It is a community where those who are leaders are called to exercise their leadership in the form of pastoral care. But leaders also remain disciples and for Peter himself discipleship within that community will lead finally to the laying down of his life. All share regardless the commandment to follow the way of Jesus in the way of sacrificial love, however that be expressed.

The fourth Gospel really ends here and there can be no doubt that we have moved into the era of the Church – the life of the community of believers for whom the gospel has been written. We are left with words and phrases like *love, feed my sheep* and *follow me*. Jesus himself does not simply come back to life, rather he goes on ahead of us into a fuller dimension of life. When he says *follow me* surely he means for us not only to follow him in this life by sharing that defining quality of sacrificial love, but also by following him beyond death into the fuller life of union with him and with the Father.

Dogma and Experience

We are just coming to that time of the year when festivals fall thick and fast: Ascension, Pentecost, Trinity, Corpus Christi. I want to suggest that through these festivals the Church is pointing us to different aspects of the same experience. It's too neat and systematic to see them as a linear series of events that tidily take place one after the other, although that's how we tend to observe them. Rather the experience of the first apostles was so overwhelming and transformative that to describe it they were forced to employ a number of different visual images.

After the Resurrection Jesus was alive in a new way, still embodied, but now his divine nature was no longer hidden but openly revealed and demonstrated. So much so that this super-abundance of divine life overflowed into those who encountered him – it was part of their experience of the Risen Lord that the disciples felt themselves filled with the Holy Spirit. No wonder no single festival of the Church suffices to describe all this. From Easter day to Trinity Sunday we try again and again to fill out a little more of the picture – to paint more adequately the brilliant colours of this crucial and transforming experience.

Now one of the worst things we can do is reduce all this to dogma. The world does not need doctrines of Resurrection or Ascension or the Holy Spirit, but what the world does desperately need is to experience all these things. And to experience them not as past events but present realities. We follow the series of festivals through each year liturgically to stir up our sense of being witness to these things, but we are of course more than witnesses – we are ourselves made members of the mystical body of Christ and we have ourselves received the Holy Spirit. We know Jesus Christ risen and exalted and this is the Gospel we have to proclaim, and the experience we have for others to encounter.

Pentecost

The Fruit of the Spirit

We have to admit that the earliest Christians were charismatics – maybe not exactly like those charismatic Christians today but men and women whose primary focus was not an intellectual belief about God and God's action but which was rather an overwhelming sense of the presence and activity of the Spirit in the lives of Christians of their own time. They expected miracles, they expected some to have gifts of healing, they believed God guided their daily lives through the ecstatic utterances of prophets and those who had the gift of interpretation.

But equally interesting is how quickly this charismatic Church gave way to the institutional Church we recognise in our own Church today. Even by the time the first three Gospels were written, probably in the last twenty years of the first century, we can see a greater sense of the institution of the Church. And the Pastoral Epistles to Timothy and Titus and the Catholic Epistles of Peter, John, James and Jude also reflect a more structured Christian community with an ordained ministry.

Bishops are an interesting example of how a bureaucratic officer, formally elected by the community, took over the leadership formerly exercised by prophets who owed their position to their distinctive charismatic gifts. Christian history has always subsequently oscillated between the charismatic and the institutional. Movements of enthusiasm recur in most centuries, sometimes breaking away from the over institutionalised Church, like Methodism in England in the eighteenth century, and sometimes being contained within it, like the Franciscans in the thirteenth century.

But the Church has to remain by definition charismatic – when it ceases to depend on the outpouring of the Holy Spirit and the gifts associated with that outpouring then we are lost. For with the Spirit our lives are transformed and literally *inspired* – by which we are led from an act of faith in our minds to the inner knowledge and experience of God in our hearts and so to actions in harmony with God's will for us and for our world. But the strength of the institutional Church lies in her continued insistence that all who are baptised sacramentally have received the Holy Spirit, not merely some self-selecting elite.

Trinity

The History of God

The emergence of a monotheistic understanding of God is relatively easy to understand. It depends upon a degree of philosophical reflection but only at a fairly simple level. Philosophers in India and Greece alike concluded that the many Gods of popular religion were but manifestations of a single underlying divine principle. Indeed we can see something of this religious evolution of ideas in the Old Testament itself. For example the Ten Commandments teach monolatry, which means we are to worship only the Lord and no other god – the existence of other gods is not yet denied. That only comes seven hundred years later during the exile to Babylon when the prophet we know as Second Isaiah finally reaches the conclusion that the gods of Babylon are but idols, there is only one Living God.

I once asked one of our local Rabbis whether he felt closer to Islam or to Christianity, and I remember feeling rather put down when he replied without hesitation that it was Islam. After all while the Arab people also claim descent from Abraham it is we Christians who read from the Jewish scriptures in the liturgy every day and the Psalms are also part of the bedrock of Christian spirituality. But for the Rabbi the real issue was the Christian doctrine of the Trinity – he felt we have compromised on the vital principle of absolute monotheism.

The truth is that we do often use language that makes it sound as if we believe in three gods. Even Paul's words that we know as the Grace are not as careful as they might be – he uses God to refer to the Father alone – but just as there is evolution in the Old Testament period before we arrive at pure and absolute monotheism, so there is evolution in the New Testament period before we arrive at a developed doctrine of God as Trinity. But what we are dealing with in both these developments is the result of the continued reflection on human experience.

All three of the great monotheistic religions developed in a polytheistic world. This though is true of Christianity only insofar as it was to find its full development and first flowering in the Hellenistic world. But the very first people to believe in Jesus were Jews with a deeply engrained monotheistic conviction. They did not come easily to the conclusion that Jesus was God. They called him Messiah or Christ, Servant of God, Prophet, even Son of God. But certainly before the end of the first century believers found no other way of describing Jesus that was adequate to their experience of him until they were forced to say, monotheists as they were, that in him the fullness of the divine bodily dwelt.

Thinking Jews were helped towards the belief in the divinity of both Jesus and the Holy Spirit by developments that had been taking place within philosophical Judaism itself. In the Old Testament the Jewish God is always accompanied by both his Word and his Wisdom or Spirit. It is by his Word and his Spirit that he creates, it is through his Spirit that the prophets can speak his Word, and by the First century BC and in the writings of Philo of Alexandria the Word has become the principle of order and reason in the Universe.

Christian doctrine always enshrines Christian experience – not only a preserved experience of the past but an ongoing experience of God in the present. Our faith is in a God who is today our continuing creator, redeemer and sanctifier. This is not a matter of intellectual assent but rather is an existential affirmation of shared human experience.

Transfiguration

'Where there is no vision the people perish'

We are celebrating this year the millennium of the conversion of Russia. The story goes that while still a pagan, Vladimir the Prince of Kiev wanted to know what was the true religion, so he sent some of his followers to visit the various countries of the world in turn to investigate. They went first to the Moslem Bulgars of the Volga but came away dissatisfied, 'There is no joy among them,' they reported back to Vladimir, 'but mournfulness and a great smell, and there is nothing good about their system.' Travelling from the Volga to Germany and then Rome, they found the worship more satisfactory but complained that there too it was without beauty. Finally they journeyed to Constantinople and there they attended the Divine Liturgy in the Great Church of the Holy Wisdom. There at last they discovered what they desired. 'We knew not whether we were in heaven or on earth, for surely there is no such splendour or beauty anywhere on earth. We cannot describe it to you; only this we know, that God dwells there among men, and that service surpasses the worship of all other places. For we cannot forget that beauty.'

This of course is a particular account of the sense of divine presence, and we can probably call to mind our own such experiences – be they a direct religious experience of great intensity, an encounter with God's reality, presence or love, or some equally profound experience mediated by natural beauty or wonder. Now in the Old Testament we read that '*where there is no vision the people perish.*' Far more important than particular dreams, apparitions and visions in the sense of visitations from beyond normal experience is the sense of profound vision of the essential truths about God and the creation. The Old Testament itself has its own coherent understanding of the divine purpose for Israel despite there being considerable development and evolution of that vision. In the same way, the New Testament documents find their coherence in a unifying vision of God as redeemer – manifested and incarnate in Jesus Christ. We need to be familiar with these visions, but we also need to make them our own: we need our own vision, both communally as a church and individually: our own coherent and unifying sense of vision and purpose arising out of all we have inherited and our own experience of the sense of divine presence.

The Feast of the Transfiguration has an important place in the first three Gospels, although strangely it is not mentioned in the fourth Gospel, but while liturgically all other events in the life of Jesus are celebrated between Christmas and Ascension this one event is kept outside that normal cycle of feasts. It is as if this feast is not just about one event in the life-story of Jesus but rather is there as a comment upon the whole story. It is, I believe, the unifying vision of the Gospel. Like Peter, James and John we look at the man Jesus – the man they knew so well and yet failed to know, the man so like themselves and yet so very different. As Jesus is transfigured before them, they glimpse that difference, that otherness. And here is man as we were always meant to be. We are all made in the image of God, but in one way or another we all allow that image to be tarnished, disfigured. In Jesus alone is the divine image unspoilt and so in him we see man clearly reflecting the divine glory, which is the true vocation of us all. It is a savage irony that it was on this feast of the Transfiguration of our Lord that the first atomic bomb was exploded at Hiroshima, the disfigurement of man is never so clear than at times of war and violence.

On the mountain of the Transfiguration the disciples saw the inward reality of Jesus, his divine glory that had been hidden. Our so ordinary human bodies are however likewise a temple of the Holy Spirit. In our inward reality we all bear the divine image in which we were born – that image may be tarnished but it is not completely lost or destroyed. It is thus our vocation, the essential task of our lives, to recover that image which lies hidden deep within us. We must turn away from the disfigurement of selfishness and then living in the way of Jesus we shall experience our own transfiguration and come to reflect God's glory to others, releasing in them too the vision of God's glory.

Assumption

Gone to Glory

What we celebrate today is something quite central to our Christian faith, not something peripheral or un-Anglican. I should point out that the old Prayer Book observed five festivals of the Blessed Virgin Mary (her conception, her Nativity, the Annunciation, the Visitation to Elizabeth and the Purification) but the ASB [check new book] keeps only two (the nativity and the Visitation). This really does represent a failure to give the Blessed Virgin her proper place in Christian theology and devotion which not only impoverishes our religion but threatens to put all doctrine out of perspective.

The doctrine of the Assumption claims that Mary, the vessel of God's incarnation, eventually died but that her body was not corrupted in death and was assumed into the glory of the heavenly life. The Christian Church has never taught the Greek idea of the immortality of the soul but rather the very Jewish doctrine of the resurrection of the body. One of the distinguishing features of the Jewish-Christian understanding of the world is in its refusal to allow the separation of spiritual from material things, as if they were two separate realities. There is only one reality in which the spiritual and material are different aspects of the same thing. So there is no way that salvation can be purely spiritual, it has to affect our entire humanity – body, mind and spirit. Thus the whole of our humanity is redeemed in Christ and raised to the glory of Heaven; and what we look forward to in the case of every Christian who dies – that they have gone to glory – we proclaim to be already true in the case of the mother of our Lord Jesus Christ.

Of course there is little evidence of this act of bodily assumption, though it is significant that there are no relics of the body of Mary in the way there are abundantly for the other saints. The assumption of Mary is paralleled by the Old Testament description of the assumption of Elijah and there are other parallels too between these two. Mary plays in the Gospel drama a part very similar to that of Elijah in the Old Testament. The clue is in the period of one thousand, two hundred and sixty days that the woman clothed with the sun, described in Revelation chapter 12, is in the wilderness after giving birth to her Son. Elijah hid from King Ahab in the wilderness for the same period – three and a half years. Both are seen as representative figures: Mary is greeted in Gabriel's salutation that itself picks up the prophecy of Zephaniah which personifies Israel as the virgin daughter of Sion and is seen as the representative of the Chosen People. Elijah, of all God's people, came to be seen alone as faithful. In popular Jewish thought Elijah was thought of as unseen but ever at hand – at the crucifixion some say, 'wait, let us see whether Elijah will come to rescue him.' As sinless he was unspoiled by death and welcomed the souls of the righteous into heaven. He travelled the world, often in disguise, a friend to the poor and humble, a rescuer of those in danger, an enlightener of seekers after truth. Judaism made him an intermediary between heaven and earth and he continued for a time to perform this role for early Christians, with a number of churches dedicated to him. If the cult of St Elias did not survive it is not because Christians felt no need of such an intermediary but rather that they found what they needed in the person of Mary. The words that describe Elijah in Jewish legend bring us close to the Christian devotion for Mary: 'Deathless, pure and by inference without sin; triumphant over the powers of darkness; at home in the courts of heaven; no mere spirit, but body and soul complete; an active intercessor and comforter; a friend of individual mortals, close at hand in their earthly pilgrimage.'

But when we talk of assumption we must always see it and Mary herself in proper relation to the person of Jesus – and the doctrines of incarnation and atonement. The resurrection of Jesus is not an end in itself. Rather, as St Paul says, Jesus in his glorification is the first fruits of a glorified humanity, if the dead are not raised then there is no meaning to saying that Jesus is raised. When we celebrate the resurrection of Jesus therefore we celebrate the redemption of all humanity and at every funeral we can rejoice because a member of the Body of Christ has gone to glory with him who is head of the body. And pride of place among all the members of the body goes to Mary who believed even before Jesus was born, indeed by whose act of faith the very birth of Jesus and the incarnation of the Son of God became possible. Therefore we say of her what we want to say, what we will say, of all believers – that she has gone to glory.

Holy Cross Day

The Cross within

This feast of course points to the mystery of how this shameful symbol, the gallows, is the vehicle of God's work for the glory of humanity. There is, in fact, another related feast called the Invention of the Cross, observed on the 3rd of May to commemorate St Helena's discovery of the cross on which Our Lord died. That word 'invention' has changed its meaning somewhat in normal English usage so that it may seem to imply a forgery on Helena's part – certainly it seems that if all the relics of the cross were gathered together today one might have enough for Noah's ark! You may also recall Martin Luther's tart comment that Our Lord had twelve apostles and fifteen of them were buried in Germany. But that anyway would be to miss the point of relics.

The vindication of St Helena is nowhere better expressed than by Charles Williams in his 'Judgement at Chelmsford'

> *It is one thing to come to where the cross is and another to find the cross. Trials and vexations are God's way of bringing us to God's holy place; that is to say, to Jerusalem that is within our souls. You may come to this church where we are and know it, yes, and kneel and stand up in it, and say thanks to God for it, and all the while you shall be as far away from that other Jerusalem as Judas was from Christ when he shouldered him in the crowd. The Empress Helena had found a Calvary in her heart before ever she came near to it on earth. Find you the cross without you, you shall find an inestimable treasure, the wood on which our Saviour rested without resting. But find you the cross within you, and you shall find Christ himself, Christ that is the cross, and so holy, so sweet, so fresh and fragrant a cross that you should laugh to find how you mistook him.*

Harvest

Nothing is lost, all is harvest.

We do not face starvation in the prosperous West. We can joyfully give thanks to God for abundant harvests. This festival may therefore seem simple and straightforward, but of course it is more complex than that. Not only is the abundance we enjoy often at the expense of others but also what of the theological difficulties? If we thank God for good harvests, is God therefore to blame where harvests are poor? We are then in danger of imagining a despotic God who decides who will prosper and who will suffer. The same issue is raised in our prayers for those who are sick. If we thank God when someone is healed, must we also not regard God as the author of sickness and death. And if we go on to say God is not responsible for suffering, then have we not so far removed him from involvement in our world that we can no longer regard him as the source of blessings.

This is a theological problem but one where at least we can make the beginnings of an answer. The God believed in by Jews and Muslims as well as Christians is the one source of all created things. Nothing exists in our universe except by the will of God. And we can therefore say that good is willed positively by God whilst evil and suffering exist by God's permissive will – because they are the necessary corollary, the other side of the coin, of our being creatures endowed with freedom of choice. Evil then is the shadow side of the gift of freedom. We cannot be free to choose the good if we are not also free to reject it. So hand in hand with freedom comes responsibility and humanity needs a radical moral transformation to redeem our materialism and selfishness with a spiritual vision of our responsibility for the earth and all its people. Given that we have the food and the means of transportation to feed the hungry of the whole planet and do not, ultimately that must mean there is a lack of will or too much vested self interest at the root of our inaction. Were human priorities to be changed then we could truly celebrate a harvest that would respect the earth's resources and the needs of all the hungry.

Edith Sitwell once wrote that 'in the end, nothing is lost; all is harvest.' Our actions, and our inactions, always bear fruit – there is always a harvest. But it is up to us to judge whether we want ourselves to bring forth a good or a bad harvest. I suspect at the moment that the very abundance we enjoy at the expense of others is ironically a sign of a bad harvest, a judgement on the society and the people we have become. In the great scheme of things, and by the grace of God and through the action of his son, Jesus Christ, I do believe that nothing will be lost, that all will be harvested for good. But let not this spiritual optimism distract us from the very real responsibility and challenge we currently face. What kind of harvest then is to be ours?

All Saints

The foolishness of God

The saints are sometimes called the heroes of the faith, but they are very different from what we normally mean by heroes. Heroism tends to be associated with strength and courage, with brave deeds and fearless action. While there are something of these qualities in some of the saints, there are other saints who are quite the contrary – timid and fearful, defeated and humiliated. We might take as an example the patron of London, St Edward the Confessor who ruled England from 1042 to 1066. He was a weak king who never managed to establish his independence from either his own aristocracy or his Norman cousin William. He vacillated between opposing factions, failed to give the country consistent policy nor an undisputed succession to the throne. He was forced into a marriage and then refused to consummate it. So neither much of a king, nor an heroic figure. But Edward did live a life of austerity and prayer, giving generously to the poor. Holiness did not make him a good king, but then holiness is not about success nor indeed about great deeds.

The secret for me between the difference between heroism and holiness is found in what St Paul says in his first Letter to the Corinthians – *'the foolishness of God is wiser than men, and the weakness of God is stronger than men.'* The Christian insight into truth insists that in the end it isn't the powerful or rich or brilliant who most deeply affect the life of a people but rather those whose lives are marked with holiness. They may at first seem weak and even foolish but in the context of eternity they can be recognised as the ones whose influence is most real and lasting. Because of Jesus, himself a failure by worldly standards whose life ended in shameful death, we are forced to revise the criteria whereby we judge people. If we keep before us the examples of the saints then we shall always be reminded of what human virtues are in the last analysis the ones worth pursuing – holiness, goodness, patience, forbearance, endurance, faith, hope and love. For not only is God's strength made perfect in our weakness his foolishness is wiser than our wisdom, his weakness is stronger than our strength.

Remembrance

For the fallen

In the Genesis story, which may well reflect in mythic form a society rejecting human sacrifice, Abraham does not kill his own son. In the words of one of the First World War poets though, '*Abraham stayed not his hand but slew his son, and have the seed of Europe, one by one.*' And that is how it must have seemed – there in the trenches on the Somme, on the 1ˢᵗ July 1916, when 21,000 British soldiers died, mostly in a single hour, and another 40,000 casualties that day – the heaviest losses ever sustained by any army in a single day.

Christianity has usually, though not always, maintained that war can be just – or at least at times regarded it as often the lesser of two evils. But war is always compromised. There is little doubt that the Second World War was fought against great evil but though it was won the victory doomed Eastern Europe to fifty years of communist oppression and it opened the world up to the potential for nuclear holocaust. The twentieth century has been the most violent, so far, in human history and this nation continues to honour the men and women who laid down their lives in the two world wars and in subsequent conflicts around the globe. Acknowledging their sacrifice we recognise a profound debt of honour – the responsibility to cherish the principles of democracy and justice for which they died and to live lives worthy of the price paid for our freedom.

No Christian could miss the parallel to our acknowledging the sacrifice of Our Lord Jesus Christ whose death is the ransom of our lives and our freedom before God. Calvary is a cosmic battle of the Somme, the final battlefield of good and evil, in which one life is given for all. And if we recognise an obligation to men and women dead in Flanders Field or lost in the Atlantic or the jungles of Burma, should we not also acknowledge the obligation to the one who gave his life for us on Golgotha? I don't believe it morbid, as some suggest, to look back at the terrible slaughter of the past. 'To forget history is to be condemned to repeat it'. And if the men of 1914-18 wanted to protect us from the horrors they endured – as in the sentiments of the song 'Oh, we'll never tell them how terrible it was' – the fact is we should remember and we should know how terrible it was. Both to help us avoid repeating anything like it lightly but to renew our sense of gratitude and obligation and to steel our commitment to eradicate those inequalities and injustices which themselves can contribute to violence and war.

All those we remember today are part of our great Eucharistic thanksgiving for creation and redemption. Here we are all given a glimpse of our place in the great drama of salvation. We acknowledge what we owe and resolve again, as surely we must, to live the life that sacrifice has made possible. It is entirely right to link the lesser calvaries of wartime sacrifice to the great Calvary of our Lord. For both reveal the deep mystery of life laid down that life might be lived by others – life, as Jesus says, in all its fullness.

Christ the King

The King must die

Before we can fully understand the idea of Christ the King we have to explore first the context. In the Old Testament God's kingship, like his fatherhood, is seen as natural and patriarchal. As in Islam as well and like earthly kingship it is about power. God is Lord of All, nothing happens that he does not either actively or passively will, choose or permit. But in the New Testament encounter between Jesus and Pilate Jesus says his '*kingship is not of this world.*' It is not about that kind of power, rather it is about the *witness to the truth*. St John's Gospel employs the vocabulary of kingship and even describes the crucifixion in the language of a royal coronation – for this Gospel-writer Calvary is not a disaster but a triumph. Jesus is a king; and he reigns on the cross, crowned with thorns, revealing the deepest meaning of divine kingship.

If profound problems are raised by the idea of universal kingship – if God creates and is Lord of all why does he continue to permit suffering – then we see the other side of the coin when Calvary reveals to us that God does not dwell outside that pain but within it. Is this perhaps the meaning of those words in St John's Gospel that the mission of Jesus is to bear witness to the truth? What truth? The truth about the essential nature of this world, about the nature of God, his kingship and his relationship to the mystery of pain, suffering and evil.

The Revelation to St John is one of the latest of the books of the New Testament and was probably written at a time when Christians were undergoing a terrible persecution under the emperor Domitian. It is a vision of hope for those faced with terrible suffering and it admits that God's loving will is often challenged and often resisted – if God is king he is not omnipotent. His power is not that of the Old Testament but that of the Gospel. His kingship is seen in the Lamb, in the words from Ephesians, slain before the foundation of the world. For in the very act of creating a world endowed with freedom, God's indwelling of that world, the accepting of its pain, is inherent.

The truth though that Jesus bears witness to is not simply that God shares our pain but that by that indwelling there can be something in the experience of pain and suffering which is creative and transformative. It is not only God himself but also now the human person who can rise to the nobility of suffering borne, of the necessary letting go, of willing self sacrifice. It is part of the paradox of the Gospel that any who seek to save their life will lose it, and any who lose their life for the sake of Jesus and the Gospel will save it for eternal life. To Christ such a king be praise!

3. Anamnesis: on the Spiritual Life

Spiritual Survival in an ice age of the Soul

Though Don Cupitt, who was chaplain when I first went to Westcott House in Cambridge, has had a bad press it seems to me that at the heart of all his work is a deep concern for the proper evolution of Christianity to meet the distinct challenges of our time. I believe he genuinely feels the cold of our spiritual climate in his bones and he is moved by the desire to point out to us our ability to reflect on and take seriously those values which transcend materialism and selfishness. In the ice age of the soul there is still fire in every human heart and our tragedy is that we don't use it to its potential.

In Western Christianity we have made a grave error that the churches of the East have never made, we have separated theology from prayer. We do our thinking about God in an essentially philosophical framework – and that today means a framework increasingly unsympathetic to any conception of God or any sense of the sacred. And we do our theology in complete isolation from our spirituality, whereas in the Eastern Orthodox tradition a theologian is by definition a man or woman of prayer. Christian theology is not an exclusively intellectual exercise, the theologian must, as the Orthodox put it, have his or her head in the heart.

We also suffer from the tendency to separate the material from the spiritual and treat them as if they were two worlds not one. This is not though faithful to the religion of the Bible and the Christian tradition for Christianity is a sacramental religion which makes sense of material things by recognising their spiritual significance. As Laurens Van Der Post once said, 'matter is spirit seen from the outside and spirit is matter seen from the inside.' The world of material things and the world of spiritual value are never to be separated out, but so then do we also need to keep abreast in changes of understanding, both scientific and philosophical, in the way the world is seen and experienced. Teilhard de Chardin once said that 'humanity is the spearhead of the continuing process of evolution whereby all matter is called to achieve its spiritual potential.' There is responsibility as well as challenge in our task.

Living sacramentally is not simply having regard to the existence of the spiritual dimension, nor only a matter of adopting spiritual practises that foster the divine fire in our human hearts. There is also the necessity of living in a way that re-affirms the meaningfulness of life not only for ourselves but for others. The sacramental man or woman is not simply someone nourished on the Christian mysteries for the sake of their own soul's health but rather someone who, being so nourished, lives essentially for others and for the sake of others' discovery of the spiritual significance of all of life.

Return from the far country

I find I return time and again to the story of the Prodigal Son for it seems to me to be the story of everyman. Jesus tells the story of course not to make the point that riotous living leads to bankruptcy but rather that, no matter what we do, nor how stupidly we waste what we have been given, God remains constant in his love and forgiveness for us.

St Augustine wrote that *'God in whom we live and move and have our being has made us for himself so that our hearts are restless till we rest in him.'* I believe that if he can say that because God made us for himself there is a restlessness in us until we find our rest in him, it is also possible and true to say that because God made us for himself, he too is restless until we return to him. It is out of his own restlessness and longing that God never ceases to call us all into a special relationship with him.

So it's as simple as this: if God does exist and if he has made us for himself in love, then however hard we try we shall never travel so far away from him that we no longer feel his call. And when we feel in our hearts that call, however faint, then we only need to respond in love. Every time we walk up to the altar to receive communion is a sign of the journey that we are all involved in as men and women who have wandered into a far country but nevertheless realise there is a time to return home. The human race is marked out by its restlessness and its desire to be filled and fulfilled. Over the centuries that sense of hunger and longing have been explained and explored in a variety of different ways, but the story of the waiting father is still for me by far the most satisfactory explanation. We are hungry and restless because we have wandered from where we actually belong. To go back is not defeat nor regression because we go back different – no longer the rebellious child but the mature offspring who can at last appreciate and properly respond to the love of the father. This is the new way of living we must take up now. God made us all and his heart will ever be restless till we are all united in him. If and when we come to ourselves and begin this new life then one of the characteristics will be to share the divine restlessness till all find their rest, their fulfilment and their satisfaction in him.

Fain I would climb

In the Old Testament story of Elisha and the Shunammite woman, the woman asks for a son and is given one but later the boy falls sick, is brought to his mother and dies upon her lap. The woman goes to Elisha and says, *'did I ask my Lord for a son? Did I not say, do not deceive me?'* A son was more than she dared ask for but the new dimensions of joy which the boy brought her also brought the terrible agonies of bereavement and loss.

There is here a very strong parallel with the whole picture of Christian redemption. Some people prefer to live without love in order to escape the wounds of love. Not always explicitly we can in many different ways decide that life and love are too dangerous, too great a risk. Sometimes it is just the sense that life offers more than we can deal with, so we forego much potential in order to protect ourselves.

As Elisha gave her a son so God made us in his own image, calling us into sonship. We are given more than we would have dared ask for and indeed many will want to refuse what is given – the potential to be in the image of God, called into the dizzy, intoxicating heights of union with him. Nothing is condemned by the prophets so strongly as idolatry – because it is an example of humans preferring something less than their true vocation. In his 'Hymn of the Universe' Teilhard de Chardin writes, *'instinctively, like all mankind, I would rather set up my tent here below on some hill-top of my own choosing. I am afraid too, like all my fellow men, of the future too heavy with mystery and too wholly new.'*

There is a story of Sir Walter Raleigh at the Court of Elizabeth 1 writing on a window pane with a diamond ring, *'Fain would I climb, yet fear I to fall'* and the Queen herself answered him, *'if thy heart fail thee, climb not at all.'* Walter Raleigh went on to risk and to fall, but despite his end his life must rank as one of the fullest and richest in the history of the country.

Elisha gives the Shunammite woman a son, introducing her to new joys and pains and all the risks of love and life. And God makes the human in his own image, calling us into an abundance of life we wouldn't have thought to ask for. As the boy dies, so humans fall and fail. As the woman turns to Elisha so we rightly turn to our creator for restoration and help. Finally the boy in the story is restored to life but not by the waving of Elisha's staff – Elisha lowers himself on to the boy, putting his mouth on his mouth, his eyes to his eyes, his hands on his hands. And how are we restored? When God who first made us in his image lowers himself, humbling himself to be among us. As St Irenaeus wrote in the fourth century, he consecrated human life by living it – his mouth to our mouth, his eyes to our eyes and his hands to our hands – bearing all the while the wounds of love which we refused to bear.

Following our conscience

One of the most significant features of the preaching of the prophet Jeremiah is his insistence that God judges us not corporately but individually. This represents what was a very important shift in Jewish theology. Before Jeremiah, God's relationship is essentially with the nation as a whole but at a time of national crisis, brought about in part by a stubborn leadership, Jeremiah appeals to individuals to respond to God in their own way no matter what the rest of the nation choose and so he begins the process of individual responsibility which has become so important particularly in the West.

The word conscience comes from *con scientia* – meaning knowledge held in common by the traditional community and in Christendom as a whole. In the West the turning point was probably the Renaissance which exalted the freedom of the individual. When the passions of the Reformation and Counter Reformation had cooled there was no going back to the medieval world where individuals had virtually no freedom of religious choice or belief. Professor Owen Chadwick calls this the *'secularisation of the European mind.'* But neither was that the end of the story. From being about personal responsibility for our actions in the light of what is held as important by the community we have now come to a place where it is thought we can think and do what we please without reference to how others believe or behave. If this is a journey of individualism then we have travelled too far! From the only communal to the individual held within the corporate to the individual alone.

So how shall we decide what to believe and how, in the light of that, to behave? Surely our individual conscience needs to be educated. For though this isn't about blind obedience to the church and her teaching nor is it about what we want. Rather conscience is about exploring within a community of belief that stretches back over 2,000 years and today embraces a very wide range of experience and understanding. Then in the light of all that, and honestly appraising our own preferences, we can come to see God's will for us, in both faith and in action.

In my end is my beginning

In my opinion Mary Queen of Scots lived a thoroughly frivolous and selfish life but in her last imprisonment at Fotheringhay Castle took the motto '*In my end is my beginning.*' She clearly sensed that Queen Elizabeth 1st would have her put to death and seems to have recognised that by that death all her foolishness would be forgotten and a legend born of the heroic martyr-queen.

It may well though be true for us all that in our end is our beginning, in the sense that only our ultimate goal and destiny properly explains our existence. The Book of Job is a useful handbook in this matter because it addresses the question of understanding the problem of evil and suffering in a world created by a loving God. It doesn't take the easy way out of polytheism, attributing blessing to one deity and evil to another, nor its more contemporary manifestation dualism, attributing only the good things to God. It also avoids the worldly cynicism of the Book of Ecclesiastes where the preacher shrugs his shoulders and says that is just how it is, a time to be born and a time to die, a time to weep and a time to laugh, a time to love and a time to hate. If the Book of Job never solves the problem of evil it does suggest rather that there is mystery here and that the ways of God and some aspects of our world transcend the limited understanding of men and women.

Job is not the Old Testament's last word on the subject and the Hebrew Scriptures reach their most sublime insight in the writings of Second Isaiah where it is seen that sufferings, innocently endured, redeem evil and make possible a new future. God thus transforms evil into an opportunity for a good which is greater than anything that would otherwise have been possible. It is this mystery of the redemption of evil that we celebrate in every eucharist and every eucharist reminds us not only of the dimension and importance of mystery in human experience but also that God is our end as well as our beginning and it is only in the light of that and of him that we can make sense of our life.

The story-teller

The Christian in one sense is someone who has a story. Laurens Van Der Post once wrote of the Kalahari bushmen that *'the supreme expression of his spirit was in his stories. The story was his most sacred possession. These people knew what we do not: that without a story you have not got a nation or a culture or a civilisation. Without a story of your own to live you haven't got a life of your own.'*

Primitive people always lived closely to a mythology through which they understood who they were and by which they related to the world around them, to one another, to the gods. Their myths, their stories, answered their deepest questions about sorrow and death and their deepest longings about life and love. We, like them, have deep questions and longings but we have rejected or forgotten our stories.

The Christian story has at times been presented as the ultimate story, the one that explains everything, the grand narrative that covers the past, the present and the future. I want to suggest that it is probably now more helpful to see the story that Christianity offers is more the story of a journey, a journey that we are all on, in the company of the other men and women of faith. And it is a story that we contribute to and shape – because it is our story as much as theirs and as much as God's. And as with many journeys, both Chaucer's The Canterbury Tales and John Bunyan's Pilgrim's Progress here spring immediately to mind, the journey is as important as the destination. For it is how we journey and the encounters we make with others on the road that shape the experience and the narrative of the story.

We have in the end to make our own journey and to tell our own story. And this isn't about getting to the end of the journey unscathed but rather about a matter of travelling through the journey of our life open to all its adventures and its possibilities, learning from our experiences and our mistakes as well as learning from those who have something to teach us, learning what questions to ask and learning how to relate our story to the great stories of our culture and our faith. Learning above all from what we can know of the nature of our God as revealed in Jesus Christ and telling the story of his self-giving love in who we are as well as in the choices we make, in the lives we lead as well as in the stories we come to pass on to others.

4. Biographical Reflection

Foundations

(preached at St John's Wood Church after the announcement of his move to St George's Hanover Square)

Some of you will know that although I was baptised in the Church of England to which my mother's family was deeply attached, I actually first learned my Christianity in my father's Baptist Sunday School. There I learned the Bible – not in any deep way but I knew its stories thoroughly; a good foundation for later studies.

But when I was twelve, my grandfather, who was also churchwarden of the parish church, urged me to be confirmed. I don't remember much about Confirmation classes but I was given some books to read where I discovered a story that took over where the Bible left off – the story of the Church. I read about Columba and Ninian, Cuthbert and Augustine and the coming of Christianity to Anglo-Saxon England. And I discovered the Church as a living community which bridged the centuries between the biblical drama and my own time. My religious experience was both broadened and deepened as I learnt to love the language of the Book of Common Prayer, the thrilling architecture of churches and cathedrals and the devotional atmosphere of an early morning Eucharist.

When I was about sixteen I went for the first time to Mirfield – a monastery in Yorkshire, home to the Community of the Resurrection. Commemoration Day in the monastic church was quite literally mind-blowing for me: thousands of people singing chants and hymns, the ritual, the incense, the palpable fervour of belief and religious exhilaration. I went back to Mirfield on retreat and found something more inward: silence, prayer, meditation, contemplation. I had also for a time the extremism of the convert. Inevitably I decided that English non-conformity had little to offer and while I was at Westcott House Theological College in Cambridge opposed the scheme for unity with the Methodist Church that was being debated at the time. But from Westcott I went to finish my studies at Union Seminary in New York and there I found myself in a pan-protestant environment whose dominant presence was Presbyterian. Slowly I came to recognise the power of Protestant theology and scholarship, especially as represented by Germany, and I came to glimpse a vision of how much richer the Church is because of its diversity.

So there you have it: four themes which have held me from that day to this – Bible, Church, Eucharist and Prayer. In the years since my first visit to Mirfield I have studied more biblical theology, church history, sacramental theology and many schools of prayer. But it has all been a development of those themes first learned in childhood and adolescence – an exploration which I have tried my best to share with you in many sermons and study groups, conferences and retreats.

Two weeks ago I was present at a meeting of one of our Emmaus Groups. The session I attended was about the Eucharist – this sacred gathering at the heart of the Christian community where under the outward signs of bread and wine we discover the real presence of our Lord in our midst and in our hearts. I wished then I had taken with me a book I have loved since I first read it 35 years ago – Teilhard de Chardin's *Hymn of the Universe*. He writes this of receiving Holy Communion:

> I shall stretch out my hand unhesitatingly towards the fiery bread which you set before me. This bread, in which you have planted the seed of all that is to develop in the future, I recognise as containing the source and secret of that destiny you have chosen for me. To take it is, I know, to surrender myself to forces which will tear me away painfully from myself in order to drive me into danger, into laborious undertakings, into a constant renewal of ideas, into an austere detachment where my affections are concerned. To eat it is to acquire a taste and an affinity

for that which in everything is above everything – a taste and affinity which will henceforward make impossible for me all the joys by which my life has been warmed. Lord Jesus, I am willing to be possessed by you, to be bound to your body and led by its inexpressible power towards those solitary heights which by myself I should never dare to climb. Instinctively, like all mankind, I would rather set up my tent here below on some hill-top of my own choosing. I am afraid, too, like all my fellow-men, of the future too heavy with mystery and too wholly new, towards which time is driving me. Then like these I wonder seriously where life is leading me…. May this communion of bread with the Christ clothed in the powers which dilate the world free me from my timidities and my heedlessness. In the whirlpool of conflicts and energies out of which must develop my power to apprehend and experience your holy presence, I throw myself, my God, on your word. The one who is filled with an impassioned love of Jesus hidden in the forces which bring increase to the earth, them the earth will lift up, like a mother, in the immensity of her arms, and will enable them to contemplate the face of God.

Postscript

John Slater was born in Lancashire in 1945. He came to London to read theology at King's College, and completed his training for the ministry at Westcott House, Cambridge, and at Union Theological Seminary in New York, where he did a Master's degree. His time at Union was the beginning of a lifelong friendship with the United States and its people, and of his strong consciousness of the world-wide Anglican Communion. He was ordained deacon in 1970 and priest in 1971, to serve in the parish of All Saints' Margaret Street. In 1977, he was appointed to his first incumbency, as Vicar of St Saviour's Paddington. Here he acquired his beloved dog H.G.Wells who also accompanied him when, in 1981, he moved to St John's Wood, whose Vicar he was for eighteen years. He served as Area Dean of Westminster from 1992 to 2001. His lifelong interest in Christian teaching and formation was expressed in many ways: as a preacher and teacher in his own parish and beyond, as the trainer and encourager of a succession of newly ordained or more experienced curates, as the Director of Post-Ordination Training for the central area of the London Diocese, and as a leading figure in Sion College, the body created in 1630 to promote good learning and godly fellowship among the clergy of London. He was President of Sion in 1990. He was also active in the London Society of Jews and Christians, and his friendship with colleagues at the London Central Mosque and the Liberal Jewish Synagogue enabled him to play an important part in a three faiths' dialogue, which became the germ of the Three Faiths' Forum. Sabbatical leave in Jerusalem brought new friendships and an abiding love of the Holy Land and its people. In 1999, the Bishop of London recognised his outstanding service to the diocese by appointing him a Prebendary of St Paul's Cathedral. In 2001, he was appointed Rector of St George's, Hanover Square. His early death in 2003 ended a distinguished ministry, lived with great consistency within a single diocese and a single archdeaconry, but known and valued far beyond diocesan or national boundaries.

Printed in the United Kingdom
by Lightning Source UK Ltd.
120328UK00001B/244-474